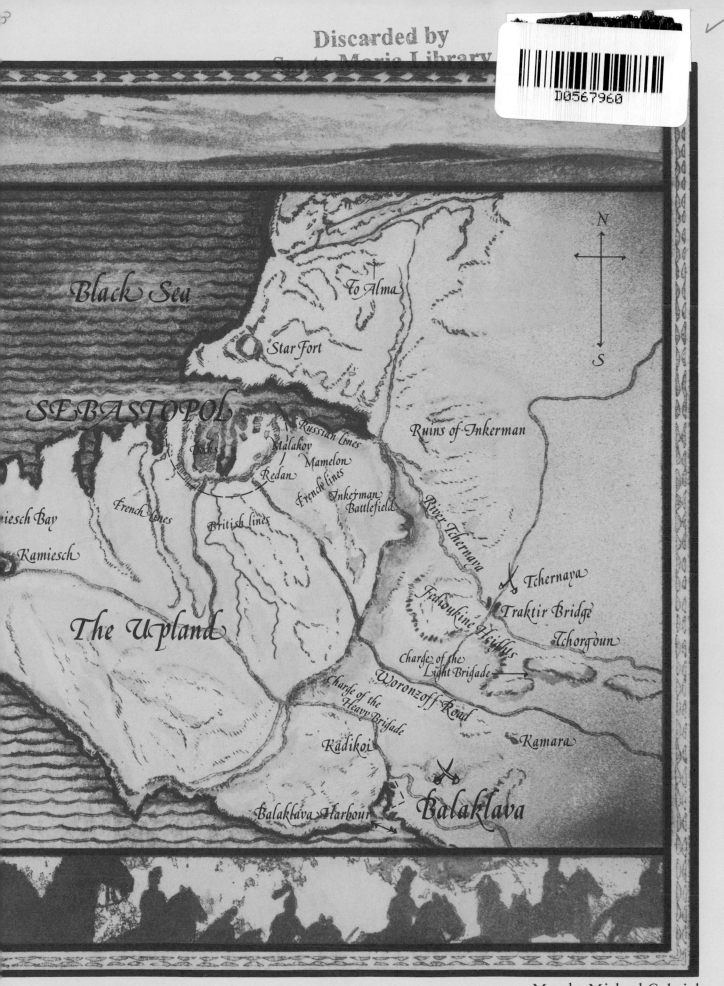

Black Sea

To Alma

Star Fort

SEBASTOPOL

Russian lines

Ruins of Inkerman

Docks

Malakov

Mamelon

Redan

French lines

Inkerman
Battlefield

French lines

British lines

River Tchernaya

...iesch Bay

Kamiesch

Tchernaya

Traktir Bridge

Fedioukine Heights

Tchorgoun

The Upland

Charge of the
Light Brigade

Woronzoff Road

Charge of the
Heavy Brigade

Kadikoi

Kamara

Balaklava Harbour

Balaklava

N

S

Map by Michael Gabriel

1854-56
Crimea

1854-56 Crimea
The war with Russia from contemporary photographs

LAWRENCE JAMES

 VAN NOSTRAND REINHOLD COMPANY
NEW YORK   CINCINNATI   TORONTO   LONDON   MELBOURNE

To my parents

PICTURE CREDITS

Photograph numbers 24, 26, 27, 28, 29, 31, 56, 57, 58, 59, 61, 62, 66, 76, 77, 78 are reproduced by gracious permission of Her Majesty Queen Elizabeth II. Numbers 1, 2, 4, 6, 8, 9, 11, 12, 13, 15, 16, 17, 18, 19, 22, 25, 32, 33, 34, 35, 36, 37, 40, 41, 42, 43, 45, 46, 47, 49, 51, 53, 55, 60, 64, 65, 67, 68, 69, 72, 73, 74 by kind permission of the National Army Museum, London. Numbers 3, 5, 7, 10, 14, 20, 21, 23, 38, 39, 44, 50, 75, 85 by kind permission of the Humanities Research Center, The University of Texas at Austin (from the Gernsheim Collection). Numbers 79, 80, 81, 82, 83, 84 by kind permission of the National Maritime Museum, London. Numbers 48, 63, 70, 71 by kind permission of the Trustees of the Estate of the 7th Duke of Newcastle deceased. Numbers 52, 54 by kind permission of the Rumanian Government.

Endpaper maps reproduced from an etching by Michael Gabriel

Copyright © 1981 by Lawrence James

Library of Congress Catalog Card Number 81–51395

ISBN 0–442–24569–6

Printed in Great Britain

Published by Van Nostrand Reinhold Company
135 West 50th Street, New York, NY 10020, U.S.A.

Van Nostrand Reinhold Limited
1410 Birchmount Road
Scarborough, Ontario M1P 2E7, Canada

16 15 14 13 12 11 10 9 8 7 6 5 4 3 2 1

Contents

Acknowledgements

I would like to thank Richard and Sarah Hayes for their encouragement and help with the preparation of this book. My grateful thanks are also due to my wife, Mary, Vivian Williams, Andrew Williams, Percy Wood and Charles Mahon for their criticisms, suggestions and advice.

I wish to express my appreciation of the courtesy and helpfulness of the staff of the photographic section of the National Maritime Museum, the librarian and staff of the National Army Museum and Gertrude Prescott of the Humanities Research Centre at the University of Texas. I owe a particular gratitude to Professor H. K. Henisch of Pennsylvania State University and Mr Constantin Săvelescu of Bucharest for their help and advice on the photographs taken by James Robertson and Carol Popp de Szathmari.

For permission to read and quote from the correspondence of Captain Cuninghame, I am indebted to members of his family and likewise for permission to quote from the notebooks of Corporal Fisher, I am indebted to his descendants, Mrs M. I. Ryder and Mr Paul Fisher. For permission to quote from the memoirs of Private Bourke I am indebted to the National Army Museum.

Chronology

1848–9		Austrian and Russian forces suppress nationalist uprisings in northern Italy, Vienna and Hungary.
1851		Great Exhibition in London. Napoleon III declares himself Emperor. Negotiations between France and Turkey over the custody of the Holy Places.
1852		French battleship *Charlemagne* visits Constantinople.
1853	*February*	Prince Menschikov's mission to Constantinople.
	June	Russian occupation of Moldavia and Wallachia.
		Anglo-French fleet moves to Besika Bay.
	October	Turkey declares war on Russia.
	November	Battle of Sinope.
1854	*January*	Allied fleets enter the Black Sea.
	March	Allies declare war on Russia.
	May–June	Allied forces arrive at Constantinople and Varna.
	July	Russians withdraw from Moldavia and Wallachia.
		Allied naval expedition to the Baltic.
	September	Landing in the Crimea.
		Battle of the Alma.
	October	Battle of Balaklava.
	November	Battle of Inkerman.
1855	*June*	Attack on the Redan.
	August	Battle of Tchernaya.
	September	Fall of Malakov and Sebastopol.
1856	*April*	Signing of Treaty of Paris.

I Photography in the Crimea

In 1854 photography was still a novelty. Three years before there had been a section of the Great Exhibition devoted to photographs and photographic equipment. Like much else in the Crystal Palace, this display aroused interest and wonderment. The photograph was another manifestation of the genius of the age by which nature was being understood, examined and harnessed for the service of man. Photography was a further example of human inventiveness and it was therefore right that it should have taken its place alongside steam ships, railways and the electric telegraph as examples of modern ingenuity. Photography could not have the same impact as these other innovations which possessed the ability to transform society, but like them it had captured and held the public imagination, and it continued to generate enthusiasm and curiosity at all levels of society.

The first photographs (Daguerreotypes) had appeared in 1839 and their precision and accuracy aroused enormous interest. The absolute truthfulness of the photograph was, perhaps, its most immediate attraction. In 1843, Elizabeth Barrett spoke for many when she claimed, 'I would rather have such a memorial to one I dearly loved, than the noblest artist's work ever produced.' Given the closeness of the Victorian family and the importance attached to family life and affections, her view of the photograph was understandable. Through the comparatively cheap means of the photograph, the likenesses of all who were cherished and loved could be precisely recorded not only for the present but for the future. The strength and persistence of popular attachment to the portrait photograph may be measured by the prodigious growth in numbers of photographic studios throughout Europe and the United States during the 1840s and 1850s.

Here lay the roots of the popular interest in photography. In 1855, sixteen years after the first photographs had appeared, Roger Fenton found himself badgered by navvies at Balaklava within days of his arrival in the Crimea. Their aim was to be photographed and their efforts were recorded by Fenton in a letter to his wife.[1] One conversation, he claimed, served for many others.

'Eh, Jem, what's that, P.H.O, to graph. Is that anything to do with the telegraph line?' 'No, they say there's a chap in there taking pictures'. 'Is there? Then he shall take mine.' A knock at the door and good pull to open it without waiting for an answer. The door being locked, there was another knock and another speech: 'Here you fellow, open the door and take my picture.' The door was opened and he was told that we were not taking portraits. 'What did you come for if your not going to take pictures? I'll have mine done, cost what it may. What's to pay?' 'It can't be done now, pay or no pay'. 'Can't it, though? I'll go to Mr Beatty and get an order for it; I'll have it, and I'd like to see the man that'll stop me, *you* won't, nor Lord Raglan himself.'

Fenton could not afford to be so dismissive, however, with the great numbers of officers who pressed him for pictures of themselves and their friends, since he relied so heavily on them for cooperation and assistance in the movement of his cumbersome gear. He took many, either singly or in groups, and with good business sense advised his sitters that they, and more importantly their families, could obtain copies for five shillings each from his London address. On 31 March, Captain Temple Godman of the 5th Dragoon Guards informed his father that Fenton, 'has also taken me and my horse (in fighting costume) and Kilburn [his groom], the latter likeness is excellent, when I can, I will tell you where to go in London for copies, as many as you please at 5s each'.[2] No doubt Captain Godman's father would have secured copies of the photograph to distribute among his family. Some of the sitters had copies made in the Crimea and sent them home with enthusiastic comments and notes of explanation (see **32**).

Captain Cuninghame of the 95th Rifles was less fortunate, for in spite of his efforts to seek out Fenton, their paths never crossed. He was forced, with the aid of a looking glass, to draw a sketch of himself which he sent home with one of his letters. Like many other officers, he had sent his family a series of vivid and detailed letters in which he described his life, friends and surroundings. A photograph was a natural complement to such information and would have been most welcome to the family of a serving soldier. There may even have been a darker side, for some of those photographed would inevitably die on the battlefield or succumb to cholera and it was therefore fitting that their families might receive photographs which showed them as they appeared in the last days of their lives.

Photography could serve other needs apart from family portraiture. It could record clearly and truly the world of nature and artifice. Ruskin, whilst sketching and noting in Venice in 1845, commented to his father that, 'Photography is a noble invention, say what they will of it. Anyone who has worked, blundered and stammered as I have done for four days, and then sees the thing he has been trying to do for so long in vain, done perfectly and faultlessly in half a minute, won't abuse it afterwards.'[3] The camera could convey information precisely and accurately and for this reason was a natural handmaiden of study. By the time of the outbreak of the Crimean War, photography had been employed to record art, nature, the lands of the Bible and the monuments of the classical past. Photographs of subjects such as these were not just the aids to scholarly enquiry, they were attractive sources of knowledge for its own sake, the means of satisfying Victorian curiosity about foreign places. Albums of such informative pictures could easily be placed as ornaments to the drawing room for casual perusal. James Robertson, later to produce a series of photographs of the Crimean war, was responsible for an album of Greek views which appeared in 1854. Well before war had broken out, the photograph was a rival to the engraving or lithograph as a source of entertainment and knowledge.

The camera might also record history. Matthew Brady, an American photographer, had taken a series of photographs of his country's leading politicians, including ex-President Jackson, during the early 1840s. He did so with the intention that such pictures would satisfy the curiosity of future generations. Events could also be photographed for the same reason. In 1848 an unknown photographer took a very successful picture of the Chartist rally at Kennington, and four years later there were less successful efforts to photograph the duke of Wellington's funeral procession. By this time there were already war pictures, a handful of the United States war with Mexico (1846–8) and the Burma War of 1852 but these were the work of men who happened, by chance, to be present. The results were interesting but not systematic. The war in the Crimea, the first major conflict between the great powers of Europe since Waterloo, offered the chance for photographers to make a wide, careful and systematic record of the campaign and the men involved in it. Such studies would fascinate the public and serve as an accurate historical record. Ideas of this sort were being canvassed well before war was declared. In January 1854, *The Practical Mechanics Journal* urged the case for employing photography 'to obtain undeniably accurate representations of the realities of war and its contingent scenery, its struggles, its failures and triumphs.'[4] With a sideways sweep at the efforts of creative artists, the writer of this article contrasted the accuracy of the photograph with 'the dimly allusive information, which alone the conventional works of the painter can convey'.

Considerations and arguments of this kind inspired a Rumanian photographer, Carol Popp de Szathmari, to take his equipment to the scene of the conflict between Turkish and Russian troops in the spring of 1854.[5] When he had taken and processed over three hundred photographs he presented albums to the Austrian Emperor, Franz-Josef, Napoleon III and Queen Victoria hoping, no doubt, to further his own career and to arouse international interest in the results of his work. His hopes were fulfilled when an exhibition of his photographs in Paris in 1855 attracted widespread curiosity and favourable comment. It was fitting that Szathmari chose to show his pictures in Paris for there had always been close cultural ties between France and its sister Latin nation, Rumania. Men of learning and art in Bucharest, once they had heard of Daguerre's invention, had shown an immediate interest in photography and quickly sent to Paris for the necessary equipment.

As elsewhere in Europe, this early interest in photography soon expanded and by the mid-1840s there were several photographic studios in Bucharest. One of these was run by Szathmari, a court painter, who used his connexions with the Rumanian aristocracy to obtain clients from diplomatic, political and military circles. It was this network of patrons that made Szathmari's venture into war photography possible. Relying on earlier contacts with the Turkish general, Omar Pasha (**51**), and the Russian commander, Prince Gorchakov, Szathmari was able to gain access to the camps of both armies and was permitted easy passage between the battle lines. Neither side seemed troubled by questions of security and each offered Szathmari every assistance. It appears that both Russians and Turks appreciated the value of his work and the generals were, perhaps, flattered by his attentions for he took care to record as many of their likenesses as he could.

The actual taking of pictures created practical problems. The bulky photographic equipment and darkroom were carried in Szathmari's carriage but this had the disadvantage of attracting often unwanted attention. When he was taking photographs at the Russians camp at Oltenitza, his carriage actually drew Turkish artillery fire, much to the distress of its owner. Roger Fenton also suffered in the same way when his van came within range of the Russian guns at Sebastopol. Still, it appears that Szathmari's policy was to get as many pictures of battles as possible and in part he was successful. Only one of his photographs has survived (**52**) the rest having been lost or destroyed; Napoleon III's collection was probably burnt when the Communards set fire to the Tuileries in 1871. Nevertheless, there is a very full description of the prints which were shown at Paris in 1855 and from this it is possible to appreciate the range of subjects. Photographs included a group of Russian staff officers watching the course of a battle, troops deploying, and the helter-skelter Russian withdrawal from Wallachia. This was not hand-to-hand fighting but it seems to have been the closest to a photograph of fighting troops that any photographer would approach before the end of the century. The rest of Szathmari's collection was more conventional, much along the lines which would be followed by Fenton and Robertson, with portraits of generals, camp scenes and groups of soldiers. One photograph, of Prince Gorchakov, was used by the *Illustrated London News* as the basis for an engraving.

The loss of nearly all Szathmari's pictures prevents any assessment of their qualities, although their vividness and excitement is attested to in extensive contemporary comment.

What was beyond question was the authenticity of the photographs as representations of war. Szathmari, close to the theatre of war and with contact among the commanders, was well fitted to attempt a systematic photographic coverage of the campaign. His own reputation was enhanced and his work demonstrated that photography had an enormous advantage over the conventional print, based on artists' sketches. In Britain the outbreak of war naturally produced a demand for prints to accompany the journalist's reports which were filling the newspapers. Captain Cuninghame commended the *Illustrated London News* for its drawings, considering some to be 'very good' but was less than lukewarm about imaginary scenes of battle. After the battle of Balaklava, he remarked,

'The pictures in the *Illustrated* of the Charge of our Cavalry, and indeed of all fights, must be drawn in London; they are as unlike the reality as possible. All a spectator sees of a battle is one line of men or horses slowly approaching another line at some distance, a few puffs of smoke every here and there and probably a few big guns firing over the heads of their own men into those of the enemy. Everything seems to be carried out in the quietest and most gentlemanlike manner, very little smoke, no dust and very little noise, just pop, pop, bang, pop, pop, pop, bang, bang, pop, and that is all.'

Whatever their accuracy, the public was anxious for pictures of the war. The first English photographer to respond to this need was James Robertson (*c.* 1813–1881), who lived at Constantinople where he was employed as chief engraver at the mint.[6] His interest in photography was several years old and he had already compiled an album of scenes from Greece. The arrival of allied troops at Constantinople in the April and May of 1854 provided him with an opportunity to take photographs (**22**). Some of his prints were sent to the *Illustrated London News* which used them as the basis for a series of engravings, adding to each the footnote that they were reproduced from 'Daguerreotypes' made by Robertson. It was then impossible to make printing blocks from photographs, but the editor's note at least assured readers of the authenticity and accuracy of the source.

Robertson, inspired perhaps by knowledge of Roger Fenton's trip to the Crimea in March 1855, followed him there in June of the same year and remained there until the summer of the following year. Sebastopol had fallen on 8–9 September and for the rest of the war, the allied forces were engaged in demolition work (**61–2**) and what amounted to garrison duties. Robertson's pictures included various scenes of camp life (**31**), but his major interest lay in collecting views of Sebastopol and its surroundings, including the sites of battles. All these he could photograph at his ease since the Russian forces had departed. He sent home prints for use by the *Illustrated London News*, but he also had an eye for the commercial value of his pictures. Some of Robertson's photographs were exhibited at Mr Kilburn's studio in London in December 1855 and a further selection appeared alongside Fenton's in an exhibition called

'Fenton's Crimean War Photographs' in April 1856. Fenton made passing mention of Robertson's work when he gave a lecture to the Photographic Society in January 1856.

Like Fenton, Robertson was taking pictures for the commercial market. This comprised people anxious to possess and examine views of the war and portraits of the men who had fought it. In one respect the early war photographs were the equivalent of the engravings which appeared in the illustrated journals or which were sold by print shops, for neither Robertson nor Fenton included any corpses or remains of corpses in their pictures although they had plenty of opportunity to have recorded them. Robertson's picture of the Redan (**64**) shows it already cleared of the human detritus which so shocked the men who had entered it within a few days of its abandonment by the Russians. In much the same way, the prints and press engravings showed battles peopled only by active, brave, fighting men. This was understandable and, given the circumstances in which the photographs were to be sold, reasonable. By contrast, the photographs of the Indian Mutiny, taken by Robertson and his associate, Felice Beato, included gibbeted corpses of mutineers, and Beato's view of one of the captured Taku forts (1860) was littered by the bodies of its defenders.

During and after the war, Robertson's pictures were overshadowed by those taken by Roger Fenton. Before he had considered an expedition to the Crimea, Fenton had become a leading figure in the world of British photography. Born in 1819, his background was a mixture of landed gentry and south Lancashire commerce. His grandfather, who died in 1840, had left property valued at about half a million pounds which included banking and cotton interests as well as a manor house and broad acres. His father, John Fenton, maintained the family's business connexion and also sat as the Whig M.P. for Rochdale from 1832 to 1841. Though not possessed of ancient blood, Fenton's background was nevertheless respectable and helps explain his cordial and easy relations with the officers of the British army in the Crimea. In 1838 he had entered University College, London, later graduated and then spent some time studying painting as a pupil of Paul Delaroche. In 1844 he turned to law and a career at the bar. During his dalliance with an artistic career (one of his paintings was called 'The Letter to Mama: what shall we write?') Fenton became interested in photography. He had been lucky enough to have been present almost at its birth, for it was Delaroche who had flamboyantly announced, 'From today painting is dead', when confronted with an early Daguerreotype. Fenton had been a founder member of the Photographic Club in 1847 and six years later he was Honorary Secretary of the Photographic Society. In this capacity he had shown Queen Victoria and Prince Albert around one of its earliest exhibitions. He had already taken pictures of the royal family and encouraged the Queen and Prince Albert in their interest in photography; both were entranced by the subject and took their own pictures.

Fenton's decision to visit the Crimea and take photographs there came at a time of national disquiet which had largely been the creation of *The Times* and its reports of the conditions of the British army. Public interest in the war was intense and this may have prompted Thomas Agnew and Son, a firm of publishers, to finance Fenton. Their purpose was commercial. Fenton was to take photographs which Agnews would sell. The obvious historical value of Fenton's proposed collection of war photographs and his previous connections with the royal family secured him the patronage of the Queen and Prince Albert. He also obtained the cooperation and patronage of the secretary of war, the duke of Newcastle. These patrons equipped Fenton with suitable letters of introduction, including one to the commander-in-chief, Lord Raglan, which helped to smooth his path when he reached the Crimea. Such backing was useful but unnecessary for Fenton soon discovered that his enterprise was kindly regarded by the officers and men of the British and French armies. Of course many of those who accommodated and assisted him did so in the anticipation of getting pictures of themselves and they were not disappointed.

Fenton, whose health suffered during his stay, remained in the Crimea from early March to the end of June 1855. He departed from Balaklava an invalid but the sea-voyage accelerated his recovery and when he arrived home, he was able to present himself and his albums for a royal audience at Osbourne. The Queen and Prince Albert were deeply interested in what they saw and heard and took about twenty of the photographs with them to Paris. There they studied them with Napoleon III and the Empress Eugenie. The French Emperor was fascinated by what he saw, and true to his unfailing interest in the world of science and invention, he invited Fenton and William Agnew to St Cloud. Chain-smoking cigarettes, the Emperor examined all of Fenton's three hundred and sixty photographs with ingenuous excitement. He insisted upon a second session and asked for copies of some pictures for himself. Later he commanded a number of French photographers to go to the Crimea and take pictures of the French forces there. His photographic acquaintance with war had an unhappy sequel. In 1859 he accompanied his forces to Piedmont and was present during several battles against the Austrians. The reality of suffering and bloodshed deeply affected him and the memory troubled him for many years after.

Fenton's photographs were intended for a much wider

audience than the rulers of Europe, and when he returned to London, an exhibition of over three hundred pictures was held in October 1855. Later the display toured the provinces, where, as in London, spectators were excited by the vividness and detail of the scenes of camp life. Considerable public interest was aroused and it was exploited through the publication of several large folios of prints from Fenton's photographs. Individual pictures were priced at between half a guinea and a guinea, according to size. A selection of a hundred and sixty was priced at sixty guineas. However, even whilst these albums were being offered for sale, public interest in the campaign was waning. The fighting had ended with the fall of Sebastopol in September 1855 and peace negotiations were concluded in the following April. At the end of 1856 Fenton's unsold stock was auctioned off along with collections of conventional engravings of the war. As a business experiment, Fenton's venture had not been a total success.

The photographs fall into several categories. There were scenes of army life at Balaklava and in the regimental camps (e.g. **72** and **36**), photographs of commanders and heroes (e.g. **1** and **21**) and small groups of officers and men. There were also pictures of battlefields whose names, such as Inkerman, were still in the public mind. Fenton also included a few *tableaux vivants*, posed studies in which a French *cantinière* offered a drink to a wounded *zouave* or a French general gestured boldly (**43**), presumably in the direction of the enemy. Like Robertson, Fenton showed no scenes of actual death although he saw plenty. Riding near to the scene of the Charge of the Heavy Brigade, he and his party came across the body of a Russian dragoon, 'lying as if he had raised himself upon his elbow, the bare skull sticking up with still enough flesh left in the muscles to prevent it falling from the shoulders'.[7] Lord Paget informed Raglan of this distressing sight and the body was consequently buried.

Here and there were horses still in a workworn and parlous condition (**5**) and dockside scenes showed apparent muddle (**70**), but there was little else which indicated the misfortunes which had vexed and weakened the army during the winter of 1854–5. By the time of Fenton's arrival in the spring of 1855, the process of reorganization and rationalization was well under way. The overall impression is of an army which seems well fed, entertained, comfortably housed and with a high morale. In a sense the camera did not lie, for Fenton's photographs accord well with the knowledge of the army which can be found in letters and memoires. Spectators who came to look at Fenton's pictures would have found nothing to provoke alarm, misgivings or consternation. It would be wrong to accuse Fenton of complacency or deceit. He photographed the army as he found it and since he had no brief to record floggings or corpses he cannot be blamed for excluding them. Later, in the American Civil War, Matthew Brady and his team would include photographs of the piles of dead and the field hospitals, but Brady did see his role as a recorder of history. So did Fenton, but with the difference that he was recording history for the entertainment and interest of his contemporaries upon whose money the success of his venture depended.

The desire to photograph the war had not been confined to enthusiastic photographers like Szathmari, Fenton and Robertson. The army authorities in 1854 were determined to possess their own record of the conflict and in May, Captain Hackett, Deputy Quartermaster-General, hired a civilian photographer, Richard Nicklin, to accompany the forces. Two assistants from the Royal Engineers, both of whom received some instruction in photography, were to go with him and he was provided with sixteen cases of equipment. What he and his helpers produced is not known. All drowned when their ship, the *Rip Van Winkle*, foundered in Balaklava harbour on 14 November 1854. Their replacements, Ensigns Brandon and Dawson, arrived in the Crimea in the spring of 1855 after having received a month's training with a firm of London photographers. Their work was retained by the army which seems to have cared little for it, since by 1869 all their photographs had become decayed. Soon after they were lost altogether. The total loss of these photographs and the fact that they do not seem to have been exhibited publicly makes any assessment of them impossible. It is likely that the pictures may have been technical in subject and concerned solely with recording types of fortifications and siege-works since a photographic course was included in the training for military engineers after the end of the Crimean War.

The process of photography taught in the engineers' course followed the same method as that used by Szathmari, Robertson and Fenton. It was known as the wet-plate process and had been developed by an Englishman, Scott Archer, in 1852. A glass plate was immersed in collodion, a solution of ether, guncotton and alcohol, which was blended with silver iodide and iodide of iron. Then the plate would be sensitized by means of a coating of a solution of distilled water and silver nitrate. The wet-plate was then placed inside the camera and the picture could be taken. At the time of its appearance, this method was acknowledged to be a major breakthrough in the taking of pictures, but it had its drawbacks. Exposure took between three and twenty seconds and then the plate had to be removed and developed in semi-darkness. The photographer had to have his dark-room close by which explains why Szathmari was accompanied by his carriage and Fenton had his specially converted wagon. The wet collodion plates remained damp and usable in England for up to ten minutes but in the heat of the Crimean summer, the time available was much less; the same heat meant that Fenton and his assistant found much discomfort when enclosed in their darkroom. So the photographer had to travel with cameras, mobile dark-room and chemicals, in all a considerable load, and bring it is as close as possible to his subject. On one occasion Fenton mentioned consuming seventeen tumblers of liquid including several of beer and champagne during one particularly oppressive day.

Given the physical difficulties of photography and the problems of climate and travel, the achievement of Szathmari, Robertson and Fenton was considerable. Through their own efforts and ingenuity, they were able to give the first systematic photographic coverage of war. The Crimean War assumes a vividness not possessed by previous conflicts. Between them they captured the essence of a war which looked back to the era of Napoleon with bright coloured uniforms, tall shakos and the panache of cavalrymen splendidly accoutred and laced; and forward to the wars of mass armies, machine-made weaponry, overwhelming fire-power and fast moving communications. The resulting photographs show a unique mixture, a juxtaposition of figures which might have appeared at Waterloo alongside men dressed for the Western Front.

National dedication

Punch's *view of the war, 6 May 1854. The caption read: 'England's War Vigil'.*

II Britain, Europe and the Crimean War

'The Crimean War . . . was merely a foolish expedition to the Black Sea, because the English people were bored by peace.' Thus Professor Trevelyan, whose judgement, frequently repeated in many forms, has become a commonplace of the history books. The war was not only lightly undertaken by Britain's rulers but it was hopelessly mismanaged by Britain's generals. The British soldier fought bravely in conditions of wretchedness and squalor, inflicted on him by commanders lacking in tactical and administrative skills. The most formidable enemy was not the Russian army but the mule-headed men who presided over a virtually unworkable system. Heroes there were, but they were not generals. They were men like W. H. Russell, *The Times* correspondent who exposed the blunders, aroused the indignation of the British public, and so began the process of reform and reorganization. There was also a heroine, Florence Nightingale, who dramatically and briskly cut through the knot of red tape which ensnared the Army's medical service. And there were stirring legends, the tenacious courage of the Alma, the Thin Red Line at Balaklava, and most celebrated of all, the Charge of the Light Brigade. These were more than tales to quicken the blood of patriots or fill the pages of anthologies of military glory, they were memorable and telling examples of the short-sightedness of those who led the armies, and, at a distance, provoked the war.

So much for what might be called the popular and simple view of the war, widely held and seldom questioned. Like all simplifications, it contains some truth and much distortion. In part it derives from the contemporary debate which raged over the conduct of the war. Not all Englishmen of the mid-nineteenth century were 'bored by peace'; a small handful, led by the pacifist politicians, Cobden and Bright, condemned the war as unnecessary and cruelly wasteful. Their arguments were drowned by the louder and almost universal noises of those who regarded the conflict as unavoidable and justified. 'We are not now engaged in the Eastern Question, but in the battle of civilization against barbarism, for the independence of Europe,' intoned the Foreign Secretary, Lord Clarendon. Timothy Gowing, the son of a Suffolk Baptist minister who had enlisted on the eve of the war saw 'Old England' in arms against 'the strongest and most subtle nation of the civilized world, that could bring into the field one million bayonets, swayed by despotic power.'[8] His widely shared view took popular visual form in the cartoons of *Punch*, where, during the spring and summer of 1854, a dedicated and armoured Britannia knelt in holy vigil, sturdy Jack Tars lambasted Russian bears, and jaunty Guardsmen drubbed wide-eyed Russian soldiers to the astonished horror of the Czar. Here was a war in which Britain and France and their Turkish allies were defending

Right, standing by international order and taking a cudgel to a brutish despotism. Buoyant with patriotism, and knowing little of the practical problems involved in waging a war, the public waited expectantly for news of victories and the speedy accomplishment of the war's objective, the capture and demolition of the great Russian naval base at Sebastopol.

Never before had the British people been so intimately involved in the conduct of a war on foreign soil. Thanks to the journalists who followed the army and were able to send back despatches by steamship, newspaper readers were able to read eyewitness accounts of the campaign. The words of W. H. Russell, printed in *The Times*, were studied with interest in tens of thousands of middle and upper class households. *Punch*, on 25 November 1854, published a drawing entitled 'Enthusiasm of Paterfamilias' in which an excited papa, wielding a poker, reads out the description of the Charge of the Light Brigade to his family (the Charge had occurred on 25 October). His young son shares his father's zest whilst mama, a hand on her anguished brow, sighs and one daughter sheds a womanly tear. There were, no doubt, maps of the Crimean Peninsula in the study, purchased from the print shops, which enabled father and son to plot the course of the campaign. Within the next few months the two would have found less and less cause for jubilation for they would have read disturbing stories of an army shattered and in disarray. Instead of tales of pluck and fortitude, father and son would have found *The Times* filled with accounts of soldiers dying, unattended, of wounds and diseases whilst the living survived without adequate food and clothing with which to resist the brief but sharp Crimean winter. Such stories were augmented by published letters from serving officers which added further details to the dismal picture.

With these revelations patriotic exultation was replaced by incredulous horror. This in turn became an angry clamour. National pride had been bruised and national honour tarnished. Those responsible needed to be exposed and hounded from their seats of power. Mothers and daughters knitted comforts for the troops or even packed hampers for their officers, whilst fathers added their voices to the general call for a new government which would tackle the problems of running the war in a sound and businesslike way. The outcry was taken up in the House of Commons and the discredited coalition of Lord Aberdeen scurried from office. In its place was a cabinet presided over by Lord Palmerston, widely believed to be the man who could put matters right. What the shocked Whig politician, Greville, had sneered at as the 'vulgar Radical press' had overthrown the government. Like many others, he feared the tone of many of the attacks on the government which had pointedly associated the shortcomings of the war with the 'aristocratic' background of those in command. Efforts to use the scandals in the Crimea as a stick with which to beat the 'aristocracy' failed. The new Prime Minister stood by his faith in the principle of aristocratic leadership, and indeed in a Commons answer cited Lord Cardigan, who had led the Charge of the Light Brigade, as a fine example of the principle's success! Still, the radicals had some satisfaction. During 1855 a Commission of Inquiry waded through evidence of mistakes and misjudgements which had hitherto marked the conduct of the war. Meanwhile, under the direction of the new government, the administrative energy and technical inventiveness of mid-Victorian England were concentrated on overcoming the difficulties of maintaining an army besieging a port over three thousand miles from England.

Even while the debate over the running of the campaign was convulsing Britain, reorganization was in hand in the Crimea. An army surgeon, George Lawson, noted in his diary on 25 February 1855 that construction of the supply railway from Balaklava was well underway, and on 1 March he commented that, 'Balaclava is improving very much in appearance, as well as sanitary condition.'[9] Transport arrangements were rationalized and food and clothing began to arrive in sufficient quantity. As the revitalized energies of the army administration began to bear fruit, the war ended. On 8 September 1855 the Russians, incapable of further resistance, abandoned Sebastopol. The allied armies remained in the Crimea until the following spring when the peace treaty was signed at Paris. The winter of 1855–6 was a contrast to its predecessor. General Sir John Ewart, then a Major with the 93rd Regiment (Sutherland Highlanders) remembered the transformation:[10]

In addition to the comfort of being in huts, the whole of the non-commissioned officers and men had been served out with fur coats and caps, also with flannel shirts, jerseys, comforters, and mits. The rations too were now most excellent, so the British army had every reason to be thankful and content.

In spite of the arguments to the contrary, the army and its commanders were not implacably hostile to reform or inseparably attached to routine. The improvements made in 1855 were not only the result of hysteria in Britain, in part they had come about as a result of an independent response to the difficulties which had been experienced at the end of 1854. Nevertheless it remains true that the industrial capabilities and administrative talents of which Britain was then justly proud did not make themselves immediately apparent when the war began.

During and after the national debate over the conduct of the war many words and more printer's ink have been used to describe the sufferings of the army and to expose those responsible. Few, save the pacifists who totally rejected the war, questioned its single objective, the taking of Sebastopol. Yet it was this purpose, decided upon by the cabinet in London, and reluctantly agreed to by Lord Raglan (1), commander-in-chief of British forces in the Near East, which directly led to the miseries endured by the army. Why then did the politicians insist upon Sebastopol even to the point of overriding the commander-in-chief and his senior officers?

The answer to this question lay in the nature and course of the diplomatic wranglings which led up to the outbreak of the war. In essence, these revolved around the efforts of the Russian Czar, Nicholas I, to obtain the goodwill and acquiescence of the rulers of Turkey. The Czar's motives were complex and far from certain, even in his own somewhat eccentric mind. When, in 1852, he began a series of manoeuvres conceived to produce a subservient Turkey he had little idea that his designs would provoke a war with Britain, France and Turkey. For him and for the Russian people the war was both unexpected and disastrous.

Nicholas I, Czar and autocrat of Russia was the absolute ruler of the Russian Empire and champion of its orthodox religion. His political views were deeply conservative and expressed themselves through his determination to maintain autocracy in Russia and stability throughout Europe. To these ends, he strenuously opposed the forces of liberalism and nationalism which had spread alarmingly through many areas of western Europe during the first part of the nineteenth century. Liberalism undermined the rights and authority of hereditary monarchs and nationalism sapped the loyalty of their subjects. The contagion had even spread to Russia, for in 1830 the Czar's Polish subjects had rebelled against his rule.

In order to preserve a Europe in which kings could rule unshackled by their subjects' opinions, Nicholas gave firm support to the conservative monarchs of Prussia and Austria. In 1848–9 his armies had put down the Hungarian nationalists, and so helped preserve the Austrian empire whose own troops were free to snuff out the liberals and nationalists in northern Italy, Vienna and Prague. A year later, the Czar had further demonstrated his faith in the Austrian Empire as the sheet anchor of a stable, conservative Europe by backing Austrian efforts to dissuade Prussia from taking the leadership of the German nationalists. These triumphs of reaction were marred by the unwelcoming meddling of the two liberal powers, Britain and France. In 1849 their joint diplomatic efforts prevented Russia and Austria from forcing the Turkish government to hand over several thousand Hungarian revolutionaries who had fled to Turkish territory. This disquieting incident showed that Britain and France were prepared to forget ancient differences and stand together as protectors of Turkey. A new pattern of international politics was emerging in which the 'conservative' powers were in conflict with the 'liberal'.

Britain and France were 'liberal' powers in so far as they possessed elected governments and permitted their subjects considerable personal freedom. Nicholas I regarded them with a mixture of puzzlement and disdain. He had visited Britain in 1844 and was perplexed by what he found. The elective parliamentary system was distressing, but far more odious to him was France, where governments were created by the violent will of the people, by revolution. The 1848 Revolution in Paris had swept to power Louis Napoleon, a child of popular insurgency whose namesake and uncle, Napoleon I, had wreaked havoc across Europe forty years before, and done much to spawn what the Czar saw as the twin evils of liberalism and nationalism. In 1851 Louis Napoleon renounced the Presidency of the French Republic which he transformed into the Second Empire with himself as Emperor. The new Emperor, Napoleon III, anxious to show the prestige of the new regime, and evoke memories of his uncle's glories, began to meddle in the affairs of Turkey. Not only was the Czar affronted by the ideas and pretensions of the new Empire, he was directly challenged by the Emperor's diplomacy.

The challenge to Russia was the decision taken by the Turkish government in 1852 by which the keeping of the Holy Places in Palestine passed from the Greek Orthodox to the Roman Catholic church. Napoleon III, mindful of the need for Catholic support within France, had upheld the claims of that church. When the Turks showed signs of double-dealing, he sent a new steam battleship, appropriately named *Charlemagne*, to Constantinople. With good reason, the Czar believed that the Turks had come to their decision under intimidation. His view was shared by a British diplomat who observed that the Turks had come to realize that 'a French fleet could beat a Russian fleet even if united with a Turkish one'. Nicholas I was determined to demonstrate the folly of such a belief, and make clear to the Turks that they needed to fear Russia not France. In order to bring the Turks to their senses and cut short their flirtation with revolutionary France, the Czar resorted to the diplomacy of the bludgeon. A Russian mission was sent to Constantinople where it demanded the restoration of the Holy Places to the Orthodox church, a Russo-Turkish defensive alliance, and the placing of all Greek Orthodox Christians within the Turkish Empire under the immediate protection of the Czar. The first two requests smacked of intimidation and the last was a cunningly contrived infringement of the Sultan's sovereignty. After all, it was argued, what would happen if the millions of Orthodox Christians called on their 'protector' in St Petersburg for help. This might soon lead to Russian troops on Turkish soil, in particular the soil of the Balkans where the greater part of the Christians lived.

The Turks refused the Russian demands. The Czar responded by sending a Russian army to occupy Moldavia and Wallachia, two of Turkey's Balkan provinces which bordered Russia. The British and French governments reacted quickly. In the summer of 1853 a squadron of British and French warships moved to the western entrance of the Dardanelles and anchored there. Their presence was simultaneously an earnest of British and French concern and a guarantee of the Straits. Turkey, emboldened by Anglo-French backing, declared war on Russia in October 1853. The Russians had miscalculated the consequences of their rashness. Throughout the summer and autumn of 1853, the Czar's diplomats negotiated in the hope that they could extricate Russia from the imbroglio without loss of face or damage to her reputation. Nicholas had blundered into the war with Turkey confident that his conservative partner, Franz-Josef of Austria, would give him every assistance. In spite of the Czar's persuasion and the memories of Russian help in 1848–9, the Austrians were far from friendly. Russian soldiers in Wallachia meant a Russian grip on the Danube, Austria's lifeline. Her response to Russian aggression and the alarming spread of Russian influence in the Balkans was the mobilization of three army corps in Southern Hungary, just over the border from Wallachia. Nicholas I was furious. He rated the Austrian Emperor as an ingrate and turned Franz-Josef's portrait to the wall, unable to look on the features of the man who had betrayed him. Russia was at war with Turkey and faced with Anglo-French hostility, and what was worse lacked friends.

Diplomatic efforts to find a compromise were rendered useless by a brief naval action at Sinope off the Turkish coast some three hundred miles to the east of Constantinople. On 30 November 1853 a squadron of Turkish warships was sunk by a superior Russian force. The Black Sea was, for the time being, a Russian lake. The strategic consequences of the Russian victory combined with widespread popular demands for firm action forced the hands of the British and French governments. In January 1854 reinforced units of the joint fleets entered the Black Sea to redress the naval imbalance and act as a check on any Russian seaborne excursion against Constantinople. The British detached the aptly named paddle-steamer, H.M.S. *Retribution*, under the command of Captain Drummond, to sail to the Russian naval Headquarters at Sebastopol where its captain delivered the Russians a stern warning. Any Russian warship which came into contact with either a British or French vessel was to return to port or face the consequences. Captain Drummond and his officers (85) also found time to make sketches and plans of the defences of Sebastopol.

Britain and France had now committed themselves to the defence of Turkey. Their warships held the Straits, and had restored equilibrium in the Black Sea. Whilst the steamships sailed around the Black Sea, tokens of Anglo-French sea-power which Russia dared not challenge, the diplomats continued to argue. On 27 February 1854 the British and French governments demanded a Russian withdrawal from Moldavia and Wallachia. It was refused. Isolated, Russia stood at bay, reminding the allies, and France in particular, of the events of 1812. At the end of March Britain and France declared war.

Diplomacy had failed and so had naval power, ever the strong arm of British influence abroad. But what was at stake? Karl Marx and the hopeful survivors of the uprisings of 1848 saw the forthcoming war as a battle of ideologies. Tyranny was at war with liberty. Such a struggle might become as a war of nationalism which could precipitate the liberation of Poland, Hungary and Italy. The demon king of reaction and oppression was being challenged, and if his power was broken, the people of Europe might grasp at freedom. One of Napoleon III's ministers also thought in such grandiose terms, and his mind harking back to 1792, spoke headily of 'the war of peoples against the kings'. Radicals in Britain and much of the public sympathized with such opinions. For them Russia was the embodiment of cruel tyranny, the land of the serf and the knout, whose armies had crushed hope and trampled on freedom. The British and French governments were not infected by such wild sentiments. Their aims were more limited and mundane. They saw only the need to curtail Russian aggression, and ensure that Russia would not continue to bully Turkey in defiance of international opinion. Both powers did not wish to stand by and permit Russia to extend its influence over Turkey and into the Mediterranean. Napoleon III, addressing the French assembly when war was declared, made clear his government's position when he claimed that 'France has as much or even more interest than England in seeing that Russian influence does not spread indefinitely to Constantinople, for to rule Constantinople is to rule over the Mediterranean.'[11]

Such were the views of the British government as well. In May 1854 British and French troops were moved to the Straits to protect Constantinople (22). This assured, the armies were shipped to Varna, a small port on the northern shore of the Black Sea. Their objective was the enforcement of their governments' demands for the evacuation of Moldavia and Wallachia. By July the likelihood of a campaign against the Russians in these provinces had disappeared. Under Omar Pasha (49), the Turks had put up a stiff resistance and the Russians retreated back over their borders. Once they had departed, the Austrian army (54) occupied Moldavia and Wallachia with allied approval. Without bloodshed and within three months of opening hostilities, Britain and France had secured two of their war aims. The Russian navy remained, anchored in Sebastopol harbour. As long as it remained there, unscathed and backed by the resources of its base, this fleet posed a threat to Constantinople. In the face of Anglo-French naval superiority in the Black Sea this threat was purely academic, but once these forces had withdrawn, the Russians were free to do as they pleased. This line of thinking infected the British press and the country's government. To ensure the future safety of Turkey, to protect the Straits, and to bring lasting peace to the Near East it was necessary to destroy Russia's naval base and dockyards (61).

Britain, as the world's greatest maritime power, was determined to draw the teeth of the Russian bear. It was not therefore surprising that Sir James Graham, the First Lord of the Admiralty, was an early and persuasive advocate of an attack on Sebastopol. Two months before war had been declared, he gave voice to his thoughts: 'Sebastopol is the key of the Black Sea . . . while the Russians hold Sebastopol, the British Naval Supremacy in the Black Sea must be regarded as temporary and unstable.'[12] During the spring and summer of 1854 the cabinet in London toyed with other schemes by which Russian influence in the area could be damaged. There was a proposal to give help to groups opposed to the Czar within Russia, and another argued for action to foment revolt among Circassian Moslem tribesmen. All were passed over and minds settled on Sebastopol. The press concurred and the public was satisfied with a war aim which would vindicate British naval power as well as chastise the aggressor. So by early August, Lord Raglan was informed of the government's decision to take the Russian fortress base. Raglan was beset by misgivings: his army was unready for such an undertaking, the French were lukewarm, and his staff were mistrustful of the plan. General Burgoyne, Raglan's chief of staff, stated that the plan was a 'most desperate undertaking' which the army, infected by cholera brought to the Near East by the French, could not, at that time, fulfil. The restrained and self-effacing Raglan suppressed his fears and gave way. So did his equally reluctant staff. These generals had been well schooled by the duke of Wellington (who had died two years before) to obey whatever the civil government ordered. It was their duty to do as the cabinet wished. They did so, and their fears were quickly realized during the campaign that followed.

The ministers and the public who called for the taking of Sebastopol were not calling for war for war's sake in unthinking reaction to years of peace. British governments and people in the nineteenth century were not pacifist, quite the contrary. Whenever British political, strategic or commercial interests were in jeopardy, the government was more than willing to employ force to maintain and defend them. The 'era of peace' before the Crimean War was a myth. In the fifteen years before the outbreak of the war, British forces had waged wars in defence of British interests in Afghanistan, China, India and South Africa. The events of 1853 and early 1854 had aroused widespread fears about Russia and her willingness to employ brute force to get her own way. Russia's forcefulness had been exposed as a bluff and her government had been forced to back-pedal once it found itself isolated.

Despite Russia's climbing down, the British and French governments wanted a guarantee that she would not resort to intimidation in the future. Russia was still in possession of the means to injure Anglo-French interests, and given her previous behaviour and the Czar's ambitions, it seemed only reasonable that her potential for making mischief should be removed. Only then could a settlement be negotiated which could lay the foundations for future stability and tranquillity in the Near East. To this end, the Allies decided to besiege Sebastopol.

With hindsight, it is possible to argue that such a settlement was unobtainable. The Treaty of Paris (1856) which ended the war insisted that Russia should be deprived of her naval facilities in the Black Sea and that the area be neutral. In 1870 Russia declared her intention to recreate her Black Sea fleet and rebuild her naval dockyards. Russia had the connivance of Prussia, and France was in process of being defeated by Prussia and her German allies. Britain could do little but acquiesce. In terms of the strategic balance of power, the Crimean War had achieved nothing. It would however be foolish to condemn the war on the grounds that those who waged it and drew up the peace treaty could not see into the future.

Whilst the loss of Sebastopol was remedied by Russia, her government could not cover over the weaknesses of her army which had been exposed by the war. Nor could the Russians hide the fact that throughout the war, they were without allies in Europe. The reforms of Alexander II and in particular his reorganization of the Russian army were efforts to re-establish Russia as a major European power, at least in the eyes of its neighbours. More importantly, the conservative axis between Russia and Austria was broken. Austria, without the backing of Russia, was left to fight alone against nationalism in Europe. In 1859 and 1866 her armies were beaten in the field by the forces of France and Piedmont and then Prussia. Italian and German nationalists were able to remove Austrian control from Central Europe and so pave the way for the unification of Italy and Germany. This was only possible once the conservative understanding between Russia and Austria had been ended. The Crimean War had ended this understanding. Russia, isolated, withdrew into itself, turning its energies to reconstruction and eventually conquest in the East. Those who had seen the Crimean War in terms of a struggle between ideologies had not been completely mistaken.

Cynical disillusion

By February 1855 Punch's *view had changed. The caption read: 'Well, Jack! Here's good news from home. We're to have a medal.'*
'That's very kind. Maybe one of these days we'll have a coat to stick it on?'

III
The Campaign
and the
British Army

The course of the Crimean War and the details of the battles which marked the siege of Sebastopol are well known and have been repeatedly chronicled.[13] The difficulties which faced the Allied expeditionary force were threefold. First, they needed a port so that the armies could be supplied and reinforcements brought to the front. Then the Allies had to occupy and defend positions from which they could bombard Sebastopol in preparation for an assault. Lastly, the Allies had to meet and overcome attacks made by Russian field armies operating in the Crimea with the intention of harrassing the besiegers and driving their forces into the sea. Each of these objectives was secured by September 1855, just less than a year after the first landings in the Crimea. Losses had been heavy but not unexpected.

Several crucial factors favoured Allied success. The hostile attitude of Austria prevented Russia from concentrating all her available forces against the Allies. In April 1854, Austria had mobilized large forces in Galicia and in the following December had signed a secret alliance with Britain and France. Her behaviour was sufficiently menacing for the Russians to keep large armies in a state of readiness in western Russia. In December 1855, when the Austrians abandoned diplomatic equivocation and actually threatened to declare war, the Russian government had little choice but to agree to terms by which the war could be ended. Further Russian forces were tied down in northern Russia as a result of the Anglo-French naval expeditions to the Baltic (**79–81**) and Gulf of Finland in the summers of 1854 and 1855. Fortifications were shelled, shipping was destroyed and small landing parties raided the Russian and Finnish coasts. These operations produced few real gains for the Allies save that they distracted the Russian government which was forced to maintain troops at places along the Baltic coast in case a full-scale landing was attempted.

What forces Russia did spare for the campaign in the Crimea were debilitated by the lack of adequate supplies, shortages of ammunition, reliance on outdated weaponry and muddle-headed leadership. Czarist Russia had always boasted of the size and invincibility of its armies which were sometimes estimated to contain just over a million men. The hollowness of these claims became quickly apparent once the Allies had established themselves in the Crimea. The major and insurmountable source of Russia's difficulties was her own backwardness. This made a prolonged war against two major powers a severe test for the government which found itself incapable of equipping, clothing and feeding even a quarter of a million soldiers. Thanks to Allied control of the Black Sea, all Russian reinforcements and supplies had to travel overland. Troops drawn from central and western Russia had to march across country, often covering hundreds of miles, whilst Allied reinforcements came by sea. By June 1855, the Russians defending Sebastopol were outnumbered. Inside the fortifications were 45,000 infantrymen supported by 9,000 naval gunners and beyond the defences was a field army of 21,000. Ranged against them were Allied forces which totalled 170,000 of whom 100,000 were French, 45,000 British and 10,000 Turks. There was also a newly arrived Italian contingent of 15,000 from the kingdom of Piedmont and Sardinia. At this time Russian sources of food were under pressure from the activities of naval landing parties which were raiding the eastern coast of the Crimea under the protection of a fleet operating in the Sea of Azov (**84**).

Russian tactics were outdated. Commanders relied upon the massed column of men as an instrument of attack. These formations, whilst formidable in appearance, were vulnerable to artillery and rifle fire. The training of the Russian soldier was dominated by drill in which the unnatural goose-step loomed large. Unthinking obedience was dunned into the soldier's mind with the encouragement of the Czar, who set great store by the possession of an army which dressed smartly and manoeuvred like a clockwork toy. Troops which looked magnificent on the parade grounds of St Petersburg found that their training was of little value on the battlefield. In terms of equipment, the Russian army was largely reliant on the smooth-bore musket which had an effective range of about a hundred and fifty yards. Against these Napoleonic relics, the British and French armies could rely on rifles which could inflict casualties at ranges of up to and beyond a thousand yards (**55**). Time and time again, Russian infantry was galled by Allied fire against which it could not retaliate. Many Russian officers recognized the poorness of their troops' weaponry but took comfort in Suvorov's absurd maxim that 'the bullet is a fool, but the bayonet a fine fellow'. Thus, the serf conscripts of the Russian army, jammed together in tight masses, lay at the mercy of British and French rifle fire.

The Russian soldier had little help from his generals. After the defeat at Inkerman in November 1854, a Russian officer lamented:[14]

It was the story of the Alma [an earlier Russian defeat] all over again, for no one knew the aim of the offensive, let alone how it was to be excuted. Columns became confused, artillery got mixed up, and the infantry, attacking without support of artillery, lost thousands of men. We did not make any use of our advantage in artillery or cavalry, none of which saw action that day. The artillery just crowded together, losing men and horses. We lost, so it is said, 12,000 men, nearly all our regimental and battalion commanders and senior officers. And all for nothing!

Of course many British officers wrote in a similar vein. Colonel Hodge (**14**), of the 4th Dragoon Guards, spoke for many when he remarked in his diary for 31 December 1854 that, 'Lord Raglan deserves no credit for the conduct of the campaign, and as to his staff they are abominable. Nothing can be worse. He abuses the cavalry and blames us for the state they are in, when it is all his own fault.'[15] At first sight the massive literature of complaint which poured from the British army during the winter of 1854–5 had much in common with its counterpart, produced by the more intelligent officers of the Russian army. There was, however, an essential difference. The chorus which sounded from the British camp was a spur for action, both by the army and the government in London. Its eventual consequence was the improvement of organization and conditions by a system which was capable of accepting criticism and acting upon it. In Russia the baleful news of setbacks and errors produced only despair, which left Czar Nicholas broken and ready for death. He died in March 1855 and bequeathed to his people the legacy of rigid and unimaginative autocracy. Russian absolutism was being tried by the test of modern war and was being found deficient. Calls for a revival of the spirit of 1812, consciously echoed when the Czar had boasted that 'Generals January and February,' i.e. the Russian winter, would overcome the Allies, were not enough. The courageous officers and soldiers of Russia lumbered into battle shackled to an administration which was quickly overstretched and broken.

The contrasts between the two sides and the advantages possessed by the Allies were recognized by Tolstoy, then an artillery officer in Sebastopol:[16]

I spent a couple of hours talking to some of the English and French casualties. Every soldier among them is proud of his position and has a sense of his value, he feels he is a positive asset to his army. He has good weapons and he knows how to use them, he is young, he has ideas about politics and art and this gives him a feeling of dignity. On our side; senseless training, useless weapons, ill treatment, delay everywhere, ignorance and shocking hygiene and food stifle the last spark of pride in a man and even give him, by comparison, too high an opinion of the enemy.

The high opinion of their foes must have been instilled in the Russian soldiers by the events which followed the Allied landings on the Crimean coast in mid-September 1854. The British and French forces disembarked onto the shores of Calamita Bay which lay to the north of Sebastopol. Their aim was to march south, gain control of a port for supply purposes and establish siege lines. The Russians, under the command of the cocksure Prince Menschikov, took up strong defensive positions along a ridge of hills beyond and above the River

Alma and blocked the Allied line of march. On 20 September, the Anglo-French army crossed the Alma and, under heavy fire, stormed the enemy's positions. Outnumbered, suffering from the effects of superior Allied rifle fire and fearful of losing their guns, the Russians withdrew into Sebastopol.

The battle of the Alma confirmed the Allies presence in the Crimea and made it imperative for the Russians to set Sebastopol in readiness for a siege. This was the immediate concern of Menschikov once he and his shaken army had entered the town. First, outer works, trenches and strongpoints were erected and dug under the direction of the shrewd Colonel Todleben and Admiral Kornilov. The Russian naval squadron, already driven into Sebastopol harbour by the larger Allied fleet, was scuttled. The wrecks of these ships, lying across the harbour entrance, formed a formidable and effective barrier to Allied warships. Civilians were evacuated and a garrison was left in the town. Menschikov, having arranged the defence of Sebastopol, marched out with his remaining troops and joined up with reserves which were then in the Crimea. His purpose was the creation of a field army which would ensure that Sebastopol remained in contact with the rest of Russia and, more importantly, provided a force with which to harry the besiegers and interrupt their operations.

Lord Raglan, his mind set on the obtainment of a suitable port through which his army could be supplied, marched southwards towards Sebastopol and then eastwards, skirting the newly built defences. His aim was to capture Balaklava (71) which possessed an excellent harbour and was conveniently close to the proposed siege lines. Raglan may well have been troubled by memories of the misfortunes which had been endured when British armies had been cut off from adequate bases or had been operating with stretched lines of communications. The fiasco at Walcheren during the Napoleonic Wars and the more recent débâcle in Afghanistan were reminders of recklessness whereas the arrangements at Lisbon, undertaken by Raglan's mentor, Wellington, served as a worthy model of sense and caution. Raglan's determination to possess Balaklava made him deaf to those who called for a bold assault on Sebastopol whilst it was still unready. The arguments of those who pressed for such a *coup de main* have been supported by hindsight which shows us that Sebastopol might easily have fallen if it had been attacked within a few days of the Alma. Raglan did not know this; he did, however, appreciate that there were still large Russian forces operating in the hinterland of Sebastopol which would have been glad to take advantage of Allied rashness. Raglan anticipated a long siege and this alone made it necessary for him to obtain a port.

Balaklava and the French port of Kamiesch (77–8) were

speedily taken and occupied after a flank march to the south and east of Sebastopol. With the possession of these two ports and the knowledge of total naval supremacy in the Black Sea, the Allies were able to begin the siege without fears of being cut off from vital supplies of men, weapons, ammunition and food. Work began on digging trenches and building earthworks for gun batteries at the beginning of October. On 17 October, the first serious bombardment of Sebastopol and its outer defences was opened. At the same time British and French warships engaged the town's seaward defences but their fire made little impression and they called off after having suffered considerable damage from Russian counter-fire. The war was already taking the form it would follow for the next eleven months: a protracted artillery duel punctuated by sallies and counter-sallies between troops in the opposing trenches and earthworks. The Allied intention was simple, the gradual destruction of the Russian batteries and their defences prior to an assault by infantry.

The Russian commanders were set upon breaking the siege by means of offensives undertaken by the field army based in the northern and central parts of the Crimea. The most serious of these offensives were the attacks which were beaten off at the battles of Balaklava, Inkerman and Tchernaya. On each occasion large concentrations of Russian troops attacked the Allies in the hope of dislodging them from their positions and so breaking up the siege. They all failed and the pressure on Sebastopol remained. Surrounded and subjected to an increasingly heavy and intensive bombardment from reinforced batteries, Sebastopol had no alternative but to surrender in spite of the fortitude and stubbornness of its defenders.

The first Russian offensive was launched on 25 October 1854 and was directed against the thinly held lines which protected Balaklava harbour. A force of 22,000 infantry, 3,400 cavalry and 78 guns crossed the Tchernaya river and advanced on Balaklava. The initial surprise of the attack permitted the Russians to take several Turkish batteries but their cavalry advance was blocked by the 93rd Highlanders under Sir Colin Campbell (4). The Russian cavalry was mauled by the British Heavy Cavalry (7–8) under General Scarlett (3) which rode uphill and scattered a numerically superior force of hussars and lancers. The climax of the action was the Charge of the Light Brigade (9, 10 and 11). Leaving aside the muddle of the original orders and the subsequent vinegary recriminations between the commanders involved, the Charge had very little influence on the outcome of battle, save that its rashness left the Russians bewildered and unnerved. Given the circumstances and the odds, the casualties were not great: out of just over 660 horsemen, 113 were killed, 134 were wounded and 45 were captured by the

Russians who later exchanged them. The horses suffered grievously, for 475 were either killed or put down afterwards. Nevertheless the action overshadowed all others during the war and depending upon personal prejudice, may be interpreted as a stirring tale of British pluck or a dismal monument to military inbecility.[17]

The Russian plan to take Balaklava and sever the British lines of communication failed. With its ports open, the Allied army could expect a steady and unimpeded flow of men and material for the siege. It was a matter of time before the Russian army, dependent on reinforcements which had to come overland and on foot, was outnumbered. In the early winter of 1854, the Russians still possessed a superiority in numbers and to exploit this, Menschikov attempted a second offensive at the beginning of November. His fumbling direction and the appalling conditions did not favour the attack which began on the morning of 5 November. The Russian army launched a two-pronged assault on unsuspecting British forces occupying high ground above the village of Inkerman (67). The battle which followed was a series of savage hand-to-hand struggles in the fog. This was the 'Soldier's Battle' over which generals had very little control, and junior officers and N.C.Os commanded fragmented units in an ebb and flow of fighting with rifle butt and bayonet. The dogged pertinacity of the British infantry did, however, owe something to the ebullient and forceful General Pennefather (5) who was determined to hold every inch of his ground. At a crucial moment, the British line was stiffened by an influx of French, including a battalion of zouaves (46) at whose head danced a pretty *vivandière* (47). The Russians, facing a desperate defence and hampered by their own lack of coherent orders, fell back. The struggle had been ferocious and the piles of dead drew from General Bosquet (43) the comment, 'Quel abbatoir!'

For the Russians, the defeat was a further setback and a disgrace; two of the Czar's sons had joined the army and this was their 'blooding'. Menschikov, quick to scatter blame on all but himself, was replaced by Prince Gorchakov and in St Petersburg the court was overhung with gloom. Balaklava and Inkerman had ensured that the Allies would remain in the Crimea and that the siege would continue. The spring and summer of 1855 saw a flow of British, French and Piedmontese reinforcements into the Crimea and the intensification of the bombardment of Sebastopol. In spite of the mobilization of peasant militiamen, the Russian army was outnumbered, but this did not deter the new Czar, Alexander II, from pressing for a fresh offensive. He squashed the objections of the more realistic Gorchakov and on 16 August, the Russians attacked the French and Piedmontese positions on the Fediukine

Heights. The battle of Tchernaya (69) was the last fling of the Russian field army which was driven off after meeting heavy fire from the French and Piedmontese. Gorchakov could not continue an unequal fight and the day after the battle he predicted that 'the renewal of the terrible bombardment will soon force us to evacuate Sebastopol'.

Gorchakov's prediction was proved correct. The defenders of Sebastopol had already, on 18 June, been forced to surrender the Mamelon, an outer fort which was taken by the French. On the same day, the British attack on the Redan had been beaten off with heavy losses (38, 39 and 63). On 8 September 1855, less than a month after the battle of Tchernaya, French zouaves (46) poured from their sap trench and ran the twenty-five yards to the Malakov, seizing it from the startled Russians. The raising of the tricolor over the Malakov fort was the signal for a British assault on its sister, the Redan. This attack was less successful and the handful of soldiers who were able to reach the fort were driven out by a Russian counter-attack. The Malakov was, as the French had argued, the lynchpin of Sebastopol's defences, and its capture gave the Russians no choice but to abandon the town on the night of 8–9 September.

Once Sebastopol had fallen, the British army and its commanders could look back over the campaign with mixed feelings. Its soldiers had behaved with fortitude and courage and its officers had shown coolness and determination. The campaign had, in the eyes of the public, been overshadowed by the misfortunes of the Crimean winter. This had not been particularly severe by Russian standards and had been short, lasting from mid-November to mid-January. It had coincided with an almost total breakdown of the army's ancillary services, and the resulting chaos and suffering had been described in great detail by Russell for *The Times.* His reports lingered over the undeniable suffering of the men, worn out by labour in the trenches and carrying supplies from Balaklava, the chronic shortages of food and fodder, and the miseries of the sick and dying who lacked adequate medical attention. All this was the consequence of a creaky bureaucracy, lacking imagination, laöcooned in red tape and presided over by iron-witted generals. In fairness, the army's supply and medical services were, from the onset of the campaign, inadequate for the task they had been set. They had been the victims of twenty years of government economy, ruthlessly carried out by a succession of ministries wedded to the idea that the armed services could be run on the cheap. This much was recognized by one serving officer: [18]

The fact is that a grave and inexcusable fault lies with the English people in ignoring as they virtually do, in time of peace, the existence of a standing army, reducing every department to the lowest possible state, and yet engaging in a Continental war on a gigantic scale.

Politicians and the public which had supported them and their policies escaped blame which was placed on the shoulders of the commanders and in particular Lord Raglan, lampooned in a *Punch* cartoon as dozing general, asleep and indifferent to the muddle around him. By the end of January 1855, supplies were flowing into Balaklava (much had been lost, through no fault of the system, by the great storm of 14 November 1854 in which twenty-one supply ships had sunk), and the administration was being revitalized. The abundance of warm clothing (**15–16**), the railway line, the huts and Florence Nightingale's nurses were the highlights of the changes which quickly transformed the health, well-being and morale of the army. On 8 March, Captain Portal of the 4th Light Dragoons buoyantly wrote home of the coming of warm (soon oppressively hot) weather:[19]

. . . all our winter clothing is cast off, and we shall soon be calling out for the lightest garments to be sent to us . . . Our men are now all in huts, and have plenty to eat and drink of every kind.

Yet he did, like many other chagrined British officers, look admiringly at the way in which the French army organized itself; for the victors of Waterloo, the efficiency of the old enemy was somewhat galling (**78**).

The army which had fought the campaign in the Crimea was neither a mirror nor a microcosm of the society which had celebrated its victories and lamented its shortcomings. Its officers were 'gentleman' and its ranks, for the greater part, were drawn from the labouring classes. Contemporaries easily recognized the 'gentleman', praised his worth and appreciated his virtues, but they found it less than easy to define him. His qualities were acquired by birth, upbringing and education, or even by habit. On an elevated level, Thomas Arnold argued for the spirit of nobility with its generosity of outlook and high sense of public duty, governed by Christian values. Such qualities marked out the gentleman as a man fit to govern and could be set against the more selfish attributes of those who lived for and by commerce. On a practical level, society acknowledged the gentleman by his demeanour and carriage, both the characteristics of birth and upbringing. Whether such men were attached to the virtues attributed to them by Arnold and others was of secondary importance. In mid-Victorian society and government, such men dominated, although they could not rule without being sensitive to the wishes and interests of other classes who were already challenging their political power.

An army officer was expected to be a gentleman and most of them were. Along with the Anglican church, the bar and the magistracy, the army was controlled by men who were gentlemen and whose background was predominantly landowning. Nearly half the generals in 1854 came from backgrounds connected with the peerage and the county gentry and about a third of the colonels were drawn from this area of society. Commissions were purchased, the prices paid being fixed by a scale drawn up by the army. Prices in the infantry were lower than those in the cavalry. A cornet in a foot regiment (the most junior rank) cost £450, a lieutenantcy £700, a captaincy £1,800, a majority £3,200 and a Lieutenant Colonelcy £4,500. In the cavalry the costs ranged from £840 to £6,175. In all cases the actual price paid was higher, in the cavalry often twice the regulation. During the war the government insisted on the fixed price, much to the irritation of many officers serving in the Crimea (8) who wished to sell out and return home but not make a loss. Over and above the cost of purchase was the need for a private income, at least £150 a year in the infantry and £700 in the cavalry to which could be added sums for the buying of uniforms and chargers.

As well as the financial hurdles which limited membership of the officer corps, there were less well defined social ones. Whilst the officers' mess was, by custom, a convivial and cordial club, its members were bound by unwritten codes of honour and standards of behaviour. From time to time cases occurred when one or more officers suffered insults and bullying at the hands of their fellows on the grounds of their unsuitability for the mess. In 1854 one of these scandals was publicized after incidents in the 46th Regiment (33) and an indication of the nature of the persecution meted out can be gained from the memoires of a cavalry officer:[20]

Well, supposing, as was sometimes the case, a new man was gazetted to a regiment, and was found to be a wrong 'un, or even only quite out of touch with the other officers, being short of class, or socially unfit, or for other reasons, of which they only could be best judges, one had no remedy with the authorities, and if one did'nt want to be burdened with the chap for ever, one had to take the law into one's own hands, and get rid of him by any means in one's power . . .
He was never allowed to go to sleep, except in a wet bed; everything he possessed was broken up; and he sometimes found himself in the horsetrough to cool his brain.

The mean of accepted behaviour varied. Thackeray's Military Snobs included the light cavalry captain whose life revolved around 'billiards, steeple-chasing, and the turf' and no doubt this 'gentleman jockey' was a frequently met type (21). Such 'heavy swells' (as they were called) with their whiskers, gambling and fast living can be seen in the cartoons of *Punch*, like the cheeroot-smoking figure who lolls by his tent and drawls to a fellow, 'I say, Old Fellah——Do you think it pwobable the Infantry will accompany us to Sebastopol.' Such figures also appeared in literature like Trollope's Sir Felix Carbery: 'a baronet, holding a commission in the Guards, and known to have a fortune left him by his father, may go very far in getting into debt . . . His life had been in every way bad.' The hard-living 'plunger' tended to be found in fashionable regiments, the Guards and the Cavalry, where his military career was the basis for his social life and was often short. Many purposely avoided active service (usually confined to India) by exchange, a system which enabled an officer to purchase into another regiment. One such was Thackeray's Ensign Famish whose mother, Lady Fanny Famish, was willing to purchase her son an exchange into a Dragoon Regiment 'which does'nt go to that odious India'.[21]

The reality was not so different from the fictional. On 15 June 1855 Captain Godman of the 5th Dragoon Guards described a visit paid to a newly arrived colleague:[22]

Sidebottom has not landed yet, but we paid him a visit, and he plied me with champagne, claret cup, punch, etc. . . . Sidebottom has brought some cartloads of boxes from Fortnum & Mason, Brook's the wine merchant, etc. and sixteen English sheep. His clothes, etc. will take at least four mules to carry, the first day's march will teach him a lesson.

Indulgent raffishness and 'high' living characterize the impressions of junior officers' lives given by satirists and novelists, but this picture was inevitably exaggerated. Alongside it might be set the impressions given by the officers' own letters, diaries and memoires. A great number, from all sorts of regiments, were careful in their duties, concerned over the well-being of their men and civil in their conduct to all ranks.

The senior command in the army was shared between a number of old men as a result of a system of appointment by seniority. Many Crimean commanders (**4** and **5**) had first seen action in the Peninsular War and were men in their sixties and even seventies. In manner and attitude they varied from the 'buff and blue' Tories like Scarlett (**3**), through stiff-necked veterans like Garrett (**33**) to intelligent eccentrics like De Lacy Evans (**2**). *En masse* and in particular, they were pilloried by Thackeray in the figure of Lieutenant General Sir George Granby Tufto:

. . . Sir George is a greater ass at sixty-eight than he was when he first entered the army at fifteen. He distinguished himself everywhere; this name is mentioned with praise in a score of Gazettes; he is the

man, in fact, whose padded breast, twinkling over with innumerable decorations, has already been introduced to the reader. It is difficult to say what virtues this prosperous gentleman possesses. He never read a book in his life, and with his purple, old gouty fingers, still writes a schoolboy hand.
. . . He is selfish, brutal, passionate, and a glutton. It is curious to mark him at table, and see him heaving in his waistband, his little bloodshot eyes gloating over his meal. He swears considerably in his talk, and tells filthy garrison stories after dinner.

The army too was concerned over its General Tuftos, and on the eve of the Crimea a commission investigated promotion and in particular the growing ranks of aging senior officers. The committee members, including several generals, were alarmed by the possibility of these old war-horses on the battlefield. Remembering the comparative youth of Wellington's staff, it was argued that adjustments in the method of promotion were an 'urgent necessity'. Officers 'possessing both the physical and mental qualifications' for active command in the field were desperately required. These misgivings were soon given substance once the war had begun. They were also rather brutally echoed in the asides and comments of many junior officers who were quick to voice their contempt for the inadequacies of their superiors.

The rank and file of the British army in 1854 was drawn from the working men of the countryside and cities. Nearly all joined as a result of unemployment and hunger. Recruiting sergeants and regimental officers preferred to secure farm labourers who usually proved sounder in body, stronger and more biddable to discipline than townsmen. Since 1847 those seduced by the recruiting sergeant's patter had had to sign on for ten years in the infantry or twelve in the cavalry. Although there were always hopes that the 'better sort' of labouring man might be tempted into the ranks, the soldier's pay compared poorly with that offered even to unskilled men. One shilling a day was offered to infantrymen and one shilling and three-pence to cavalrymen but various deductions for uniform and victuals could reduce this by half or two-thirds.

In peace-time, the soldier lived in barracks which ranged widely in condition and comfort. Six out of every one hundred men were allowed to keep their wives and families in the barracks, often sharing sleeping quarters with their unmarried colleagues. Some of these wives (13–14) earned four or five shillings a week for washing and cleaning and they could and did follow their husbands on campaign, much as they had done in the Peninsular war forty years before.

The mid-Victorian public looked somewhat askance at the moral tone of its army which was widely regarded as an institution by which brutal men became more brutal. The soldier was a slave to strong drink, foul language and brawling. Like others from his class, he could be persuaded to renounce his vices and at least be put in the way of improvement. Long before the war began, many regimental commanders had taken the initiative in providing libraries, savings banks and recreation rooms for their men. Habits of temperance and thrift were not completely absent from many recruits whose background had been 'respectable' in so far as they possessed some education and a trade. The well known view of the army given by Timothy Gowing is in a way unrepresentative since he was a minister's son, literate and sensitive to the bad habits of some of his colleagues.[24] For instance he emphasized, in his reminiscences, the connexion between drunkenness and sickness, alleging that the drunkards suffered heavily from illnesses which might have been avoided had they been more abstemious. Gowing also described, with some fervour, his encounter with Captain Hedley Vicars, the evangelical officer who made strenuous and sincere efforts to convert his men. Vicars's talks with his men about God and his prayer meetings may have drawn disapproving remarks from more conventional officers but they pointed the way towards the future. In the years after the Crimea, government and officers would take many measures designed to improve the quality of the soldier's life as well as the overall moral tone of the army.

One widely recognized token of the brutality of army life was the continued reliance on flogging as a means of punishment. An anti-flogging lobby had been in existence for some time and drew strength from much publicized reports of fatalities during the 1830s and 1840s. The army authorities resisted moves for its abolition, but in 1852 the maximum number had been reduced to forty-five strokes, the force of the blows depending on the inclination of the drummers called to carry out the sentence and the intensity of rage of the commanding officer (17). Many officers found the punishment distasteful and cruel whilst others regarded it as essential for the discipline of the service. Corporal Fisher of the 95th remarked on the increase of flogging during the campaign before Sebastopol and also the general delight when his colonel, a stern believer in flogging, was replaced by a more moderate man.[25] Nevertheless, Fisher recognized that flogging was a necessity in the army although he considered that it should only be resorted to 'with caution'. His view prevailed and flogging was retained as a means of punishment until 1881 in spite of public protest to the contrary. It is however worth noting that the public willingly accepted the institution of flogging for criminals guilty of robbery with violence in 1861.

As might be expected, soldiers' memoires are rarer than officers and so it is not easy to assess their feelings towards their superiors. That a gulf existed there was no doubt even though a handful of other ranks, usually N.C.Os, were given commissions. This habit, regretted by the duke of Wellington on the grounds that the ex-ranker would naturally be ill at ease in the mess and unable to share the pastimes of its normal members, was still uncommon. As one officer remarked, echoing the opinions of Wellington, promotion from the ranks was doomed to failure for the new arrival in the mess would find himself isolated by accent and bearing from his colleagues. Such views may seem savage but they are well represented in the literature of the period, especially the novels of Trollope, which often revolve around the preciseness and niceties of social division and the most ill-defined and yet insurmountable barrier of all, that between the gentleman and non-gentleman.

For the army in the Crimea, the war had two major results. The culminative effects of years of neglect and ministerial cheese-paring were recognized and measures taken to rectify them. The process of reform, always rather slow in Victorian Britain, was accelerated and its consequence was a rationalization of the administration and the overall betterment of the soldier's lot. Public indifference and hostility towards the army was swept away. The public was able to follow the detail of the war in a way which aroused its enthusiasm, anger and compassion. Thanks to the steamship, the telegraph, the press and the camera, battlefields and the men who fought on them were brought close to the public. The courage of the army stirred national, patriotic fervour. Charles Kingsley, apostle of manly patriotism, retelling the story of the Argonauts in *The Heroes* (1855) drew his young readers' attention to the similarities between the high-minded adventurers of legend and their contemporary counterparts:

And there are heroes in our days also, who do noble deeds, but not for gold. Our discoverers did not go to make themselves rich when they sailed out one after another into the dreary frozen seas; nor did the ladies who went out last year to drudge in the hospitals of the East, making themselves poor, that they might be rich in noble works. And young men too, whom you know, children, and some of them your own kin, did they say to themselves, 'How much money shall I earn?' when they went out to the war, leaving wealth, and comfort, and a pleasant home, and all that money can give, to face hunger and thirst, and wounds and death, that they might fight for their country and their Queen?

So the heroes of the Alma, Balaklava, Inkerman and the Redan joined the worthies of past, united in loftiness of ambition and sacrifice. History cannot be written in the subjunctive, but it would be interesting to wonder what comments Kingsley's sentiments would have drawn from the men themselves.

The Photographs

1. Leaders

1. Fitzroy Somerset, Lord Raglan (1788–1855) *(Fenton)*

Raglan, who had lost his right arm at Waterloo, bore the brunt of press criticism of the conduct of the war even though he had warned the government of the army's unpreparedness for the expedition to the Crimea.

Lord Raglan rode through our camp this afternoon [following the Charge of the Light Brigade], *which caused some excitement among the fellows, rushing out to cheer him in their shirt sleeves. But he did not say anything. How I longed for him to do so, as I walked by his horse's head! One little word, 'Well, my boys, you have done well', or anything of the sort, would have cheered us all up, but then it would have entailed on him more cheers, which would have been distasteful to him; more's the pity, though one cannot but admire such a nature* (Lord George Paget, 4th Light Dragoons).

How bitterly The Times and other papers are beginning to abuse poor old Raglan. Man is a regular contrary animal and I suppose it is for that reason that I who abused him myself a little time ago begin to think that he is a little hardly used or at least the newspapers should not be allowed to write in such terms of any man holding the position of Commander-in-Chief especially in the field. There is however a great deal of truth in what they say. He is no doubt a shocking old muff and also very sensitive to the weight of newspaper censure. Since the Article in The Times about the invisible Commander-in-Chief he has been riding about the lines in a most frantic way making himself obnoxious in every direction (Captain Cuninghame, 95th Rifles, 19 January 1855).

2. General Sir George de Lacy Evans (1787–1870) *(Fenton)*

De Lacy Evans was commissioned in 1807 and saw action in India, in the Peninsular War, and in the United States where he took part in the campaign against Washington and was wounded at the battle of New Orleans. He was present at Waterloo where he served on General Picton's staff and is supposed to have carried the order for the charge of the Union Brigade. In 1835 he accepted command of the British legion which fought for Queen Christina of Spain against the reactionary Carlists – one of the large medals on his chest is probably the Grand Cross of the Order of St Ferdinand and Charles III, awarded him by a grateful Spanish government.

De Lacy Evans was a radical reformer who had entered politics in 1831 as M.P. for Rye. In 1832 he stood for Westminster as a radical and won the seat which he held (with a five-year break) until 1865 when he resigned from political life.

In the Crimea, de Lacy Evans commanded the Second Division and was wounded at the Alma. At nearly seventy years of age, he remained a courageous, intelligent and popular commander, but his service in the Crimea was marred by ill-health which eventually forced his return to England.

3. General Sir James Scarlett (1799–1871) *(Fenton)*

In 1854 Scarlett was appointed commander of the Heavy Cavalry Brigade and in the following year he was given overall command of the British cavalry. The son of a highly successful lawyer, Scarlett proceeded through Eton and Trinity College, Cambridge to a commission in the 18th Hussars at the age of nineteen. From 1836 to 1841 he was Tory M.P. for Guildford, saying little in debates but regularly helping his party in the lobbies.

On 25 October 1854 he commanded and led the heavy cavalry squadrons (7 and 8) in the Charge of the Heavy Brigade during the battle of Balaklava: British horsemen successfully charged uphill and scattered a larger force of Russian Hussars and Lancers. Scarlett, wearing his brass dragoon helmet, ordered the charge and was the first into the Russian ranks.

4. General Sir Colin Campbell (1792–1863) *(Fenton)*

The son of a Glasgow carpenter, Campbell was commissioned in 1807 and served under Sir John Moore in the Peninsula. In the Crimea, he commanded the Highland Brigade on the condition that he was permitted to wear the feathered Highland bonnet, which he seems to have abandoned by the time this picture was taken. At Balaklava, he commanded the 93rd Highlanders in the brief action which came to be known as the 'Thin Red Line'. The Highlanders stood between Balaklava Harbour and four squadrons of Russian Hussars. Sir Colin coolly drew up his 550 men into two lines and bluntly warned them, *'Remember there is no retreat from here, men! You must die where you stand!' 'Ay, ay, Sir Colin; we'll do that'*, was at least one reply. Two volleys were fired at the Russians who wheeled and galloped off. Their officers, perplexed by the Highlanders' stand, wrongly imagined that they were supported and accordingly withdrew. Few Russians died, but the firmness of the Highlanders and W. H. Russell's journalistic flourish 'the thin red streak' (amended in 1877 to 'thin red line') turned the incident into a legend.

Campbell again commanded his Highlanders in the Indian Mutiny (1857) when he led the column which relieved Lucknow.

5. General Sir John Lysaght Pennefather (1800–1872) with Light Dragoon orderly *(Fenton)*

Pennefather commanded the 4th Division at Inkerman (5 November 1854) where, at one stage, he faced 35,000 Russian infantry with a tenth of that number. Determined not to give an inch of ground, he rode about in the fog, encouraging his men with a smile and more frequently with ferocious oaths and curses. When the Russians seemed to be falling back, he pleaded with Raglan for more men so that he could pursue *'and lick them to the devil.'* His pugnacity drew approving remarks from the French Marshal Canrobert who commented, *'Ah! quel brave garçon! quel brave homme! quel bon géneral!'* Pennefather's characteristic summary of the battle was, *'I tell you, we gave 'em a hell of a towelling.'*

The orderly, who wears the uniform of a trooper of the 4th Light Dragoons, looks much as his colleagues must have done when they charged with the Light Brigade. His rather lack-lustre horse seems to have suffered badly during the rigours of the previous winter.

6. Lord George Paget (1818–1880), Colonel 4th Light Dragoons
(Fenton)

Lord Paget commanded his regiment when it charged with the
Light Brigade at Balaklava on 25 October 1854.

There was no one, I believe, who when he started on this advance, was
insensible to the desperate undertaking in which he was about to be
engaged. Ere we had advanced half our distance, bewildered horses
from the first line, riderless, rushed in upon our ranks, in every state of
mutilation, intermingled soon with riders who had been unhorsed,
some of them with a limping gait, that told too truly of their state . . .
A Lancer is now seen on our left prodding away at a dismounted
Russian officer, apparently unarmed. I holloa to let him alone, which
he obeys, though reluctantly (for their monkeys are up at this time)
(Lord George Paget, 4th Light Dragoons).

2. The British Army

7. Colonel George Clarke, Royal Scots Greys *(Fenton)*

Colonel Clarke, in winter dress and standing beside the horse, led one of the two squadrons of the Greys which charged uphill against Russian light cavalry at Balaklava. His horse 'Sultan' became over-exhilarated and rushed forward taking the Colonel into the midst of the Russians and causing him to lose his bearskin. He was cut about the head but continued to fight in the melée, which was described by a fellow officer as like *'coming in and out of a crowded theatre, jostling horse against horse, violent language, hacking and pushing, till suddenly the Russians gave way'*.

The horse, one of the lucky handful which came through the winter, is probably a regimental animal for it is branded '2D' (2nd Dragoons) on its rump.

8. Captain Adolphus Burton, 5th Dragoon Guards *(Fenton)*

Captain Burton commanded two squadrons of his regiment which charged, alongside the Scots Greys, at Balaklava. His men had suffered heavily from cholera and when command of the regiment fell upon him, he was anxious to sell his commission. Unable to get a price beyond that fixed by Army regulations, he remained in the Crimea.

He wears campaign dress, with a brass helmet (lacking the ceremonial horsehair plume), red jacket with dark green regimental facings and collar and dark blue overalls with a gold stripe.

9. Colonel Doherty, officers and men, 13th Light Dragoons
(Fenton)

This group, complete with dog, includes survivors of the Charge of the Light Brigade. Second from the left is Cornet Denzil Chamberlayne whose horse was killed. Unhurt, he removed the saddle and began to walk back to allied lines. In passing he remarked to another officer, *'another horse you can get, but you will not buy another saddle so easily.'* The Russians let him go on his way unhindered, perhaps mistaking him for a Cossack pillager.

Captain Jenyns (standing immediately above the seated figure with the dog) claimed that he saw Lord Cardigan among the Russian guns and so was drawn into the rather sour controversy as to whether the earl ever reached the Russian lines.

The sixth figure from the left is Veterinary-Surgeon Thomas Towers, who charged with the regiment and presumably took part in the killing of the many wounded horses afterwards. It was during the war that he and his like were officially permitted the status of officers and gentlemen.

10. Quartermaster John Hill, 4th Light Dragoons *(Fenton)*

A veteran of the campaigns in Afghanistan in 1838–40, Hill was present at the Charge of the Light Brigade. The horse he is sitting on may be the one he rode then, for it was, as its appearance suggests, a survivor of the winter.

11. Cornet John Wilkin, 11th Hussars *(Fenton)*

An Assistant-Surgeon, Wilkin rode with his regiment in the Charge of the Light Brigade and subsequently purchased himself the rank of Cornet. An excellent horseman, he did well in the races organized during the spring of 1855.

Wilkins [sic] *of the 11th Hussars came in first with his horse, having I am told, gone over the ground most beautifully. He seems to be very fortunate, winning nearly all the races he has ridden himself* (Staff Assistant Surgeon George Lawson).

Wilkin was one of the very few officers who posed for Fenton in full dress uniform. On his head is the fur cap (or busby after the London hatter, W. Busby) of dark brown fur with a white plume and scarlet bag. Around the busby was a gold cord which attached to the jacket. The jacket is of blue cloth with heavy gold frogging across the chest and gold lace on the sleeves. Around the waist is a sash of scarlet and gold. The overalls are crimson (hence the regimental nickname of 'Cherubims' or less politely 'Cherry Bums') with a gold stripe. The sheepskin saddle-cover was black with red edging.

12. Lieutenant Shadwell Grylls, Royal Horse Artillery
(Fenton)

Grylls was attached to 'C' Battery which supported the Heavy Brigade at Balaklava and was able to fire a few rounds into the departing Russian cavalry.

Like Wilkin (**11**), Grylls posed in parade ground order. He wears a dark blue uniform with red collar and cuffs, a yellow and red barred sash, and plenty of gold frogging. On his head is a black busby with a red sack.

13. Hut of Captain Webb, 4th Dragoon Guards *(Fenton)*

I hope that you will receive the photographic views of my hut and camp all safe. The man who did them has, I think, returned to England . . . He did a good thing of myself, Webb, Forster, sitting down at the door of his Marquee, and a white horse of Forster's being held by a servant. Then there is another [this picture] *of Webb, Forster and myself* [the frock-coated figure in the centre, standing in profile], *Mrs Rogers, and Webb's servant* [holding the pony] *and pony. We are standing at the door of Webb's hut (Colonel Hodge, 4th Dragoon Guards, 11 May 1855).*

14. Camp of the 4th Dragoon Guards *(Fenton)*

A posed scene in which some French Zouaves (on the left) share a pipe and a drink with some British officers and troopers. The lady is Mrs Rogers, the wife of a trooper in the regiment. Her duties including providing food and washing clothes and she was admired for her fortitude.

I have just been informed that a regular official application has been this day sent in by Mrs Duberly [see 39] of the 8th, signed by Colonel Shewell, applying for the Crimean Medal and clasps for Balaklava and Inkerman. I rather think that Parlby refuses to forward it, but if she gets it, I will apply for one for Mrs Rogers who deserves it ten times more than half the men who will get it (Colonel Hodge, 4th Dragoon Guards, 2 June 1855).

15. Two officers, 4th Light Dragoons *(Fenton)*

Although this and subsequent pictures were taken during the spring and summer of 1855, Fenton had persuaded the subjects to wear the clothes worn during the bitter mid-winter months of December, January and February. Unpreparedness and heavy losses of clothing when a storm destroyed ships in Balaklava in November 1855, forced soldiers to buy their own winter clothing or else rely on the scanty supplies then available.

3 January [1855] Rode into Balaklava to try to obtain a box that I heard was there for me, found it and carried it out upon my horse. On opening it I found a large fur coat, a beautiful one, but too big for me, also a fine fur cap, gloves &c., &c.,. The coat is too good. It cost £15 15shs.
   *5 January. This morning the thermometer was at 24 in my tent. Sold my fur coat to Webb (see **14**) for £16* (Colonel Hodge, 4th Dragoon Guards).

I shall now make you laugh by telling you how I am clothed to keep out the cold. First of all a red flannel shirt (sometimes two) a woollen waistcoat over that then a small Regimental jacket, & over that a short Kafir War shaped Patrol Jacket – over the whole a thick heavy cloak with sleeves. On my feet a pair of silk socks lined with wool, another pair of stout worsted going over them, with drawers & trousers then a pair of Turkish cloth slippers the whole going into a pair of large Russian leather boots, which go over trousers & all up to the knee [see figure on the left]. A stout Fur Cap on the head & fur gloves lined with wool on the hands – & with all this I assure you I am only tolerably warm (Major Richard Tylden, R.E., 18 January 1855).

16. Men of the 68th Regiment (Durham Light Infantry)
(Fenton)

By the time this picture was taken supplies of warm clothing
were reaching the Crimea in abundance.

*The fur clothing in bundles, such as sheepskin coats and buffalo robes,
should be immediately unpacked, since not only are they not completely dry, but they are liable to spontaneous combustion; I should say,
generate inflammable gases* (H. W. Gordon, Superintendent of
Collection of Clothing and Stores, 9 April 1855).

*There was now great talk of things being about to be brought up from
Balaklava such as long boots, buffalo hides, fur jackets, &c., and at last
we really had the pleasure of seeing some of these things, and we found
them very acceptable . . . We now got presents from England such as
gurnseys, comforters &c* (Corporal John Fisher, 95th Rifles).

17. Officers and men of the 89th Regiment (Royal Irish Fusiliers) *(Fenton)*

The two figures on the right wear winter dress with what appear to be prototypes of the Balaklava helmet. The standing officer on the far left, probably a recent arrival, wears the new style uniform which had been introduced in April 1855. The other officers wear loose jackets over scarlet shell jackets. The standing sergeant wears the old pattern uniform with the scarlet coatee and the universally popular Kilmarnock cap with the grenade badge to denote that he was attached to the Grenadier Company.

The uniform changes of 1855 were the consequence of several years of planning and were designed to produce a more comfortable and practical fighting dress. The colonel (seated in the middle) would, like his fellows, have been responsible for providing clothing for his regiment – an eighteenth-century custom which had been ended in June 1854.

18. Officers of the 90th Regiment (2nd Batallion, Cameronians) *(Fenton)*

Each man wears the almost standard officers' dress for the Crimea – regulation dark blue trousers and shell jackets with peaked caps (two have pairs of white gloves tucked into their jackets). They are also bearded. What *Punch* called the beard and moustache 'movements' were well under way at the beginning of 1854 and were closely identified with the more fashionable, high-living elements in the army or, in the phrase of the time, 'heavy swells'. The war gave a vigorous impetus to the movements and in spite of irritated rearguard actions by the more conservative generals, beards were given official blessing.

A large part of the Army being employed in Turkey, where it has been found beneficial to keep the upper lip unshaven and allow the moustache to grow, the General Commanding-in-Chief is pleased to authorize that practice in the Army generally, subject to the following Regulations.

A clear space of two inches must be left between the corner of the mouth and the whisker – when whiskers are grown. The chin, the under lip and at least two inches of the upper part of the throat must be clean shaven, so that no hair can be seen above the stock [leather collar, reluctantly abandoned by senior officers shortly after].

The wearing of the moustache is to be optional with all ranks (General Sir George Cathcart, 21 July 1854).

19. General Sir Henry Barnard (1799–1857) *(Fenton)*

General Barnard took command of the 3rd Division on his arrival in the Crimea in February 1855 and became Chief of Staff in the following July. A brave and courteous officer, he was well liked. The picture also shows his servant or groom (in the fur cap) and a bird cage (on the left), presumably containing the pet of the General. The kneeling figure with the kettle may possibly be Spurling, Fenton's assistant. Fenton found General Barnard agreeable and helpful and the two men dined together on several occasions.

I rode towards the front and enquired for General Barnard (Grenadier Guards) to whom Mr Angel gave me an introduction. His tent is pitched on a slope looking down towards the town [Sebastopol], *a beautiful situation. He was at lunch with another officer and made me join in, some more bacon was fried and another bottle of porter discharged its cork against the Russian batteries and we refreshed the inner man, watching the puffs of smoke as the batteries on either side discharged occasionally at each other* (Roger Fenton, 15 March 1855).

20. General Barnard's horse, the grandson of Napoleon's 'Marengo' *(Fenton)*

Infantry officers attempted, when possible, to obtain horses. Many (e.g. **32**) chose light ponies, sometimes the local Tartar breed. The General's splendid thoroughbred, here ridden by his groom or servant, was an exception if only because of his condition.

There have been so many rumours of an intended move lately that I have been frightened into what I am afraid my father will consider the unjustifiable extravagance of buying another horse, one about 15–2., handsome, nearly thoroughbred in appearance, fast, strong, fiery but gentle and perfectly broke to firearms. For this animal I was obliged to pay £50. I knew I could never get within a mile of firing on my pony. The Cossack (as my new charger is called) I intend to keep entirely as a war-horse. He is too fiery and fidgety for parades, the great point is his standing fire (Captain Cuninghame, 95th Rifles).

21. Captain Morgan, A.D.C. to General Barnard on 'Cox-comb' (Fenton)

British officers found the Crimea well suited to their sporting tastes. During the spring and summer of 1855 there was plenty of scope for riding and shooting; Colonel Hodge enjoyed fox hunting near Constantinople in the following year. There were also races, organized for the pleasure of officers and the entertainment of troops. According to Fenton, this horse was the winner of several races for its owner, General Barnard.

We had great sport here the day before yesterday, no less than the 4th Division Races! The fun we had was immense and though of course the pace was not first rate, I believed everyone enjoyed it as much if not more than any of the great English race-meetings. It was numerously attended, I should think all the officers of the Army who were not in the trenches or on duty were there, and many French officers too, mostly mounted. The scurry from the starting to the winning post to see the finish was as good as a charge of Cavalry. There were crowds of men to see the fun. The whole thing looked very much like a country race-meeting in England with a larger proportion of red-coats and fewer boys and women. The crack event of the day was won by a small middy [mid-shipman] *about 12 years old who rode over from Kherson for the purpose and who was loudly cheered on coming in miles ahead of everyone else. We are to have another day's sport next Thursday foot-racing, jumping etc., for the men, so you see with the warm weather we are also recovering our spirits. The course is in full sight of Sebastopol; I should think the Russians must have been rather astonished at witnessing such joviality* (Captain Cuninghame, 95th Rifles, 19 March 1855).

22. Grenadier Guards at Haider Pasha *(Robertson)*

Taken in late May or early June 1854, this is one of the earliest surviving photographs of the war. The Guards are in white summer service trousers with a few bearskins. The figure in civilian clothes may be an officer or Robertson's associate, Felice Beato. The two figures lying in the foreground suggest that some soldiers had adopted more fitting dress for the climate; an enterprise which was frowned upon by some officers like Sir George Brown who banned linen covers for the brass Dragoon helmets on the grounds that they were 'unsoldierlike'. A rickety cart is a token of the regiment's efforts to obtain transport. The short stay at Constantinople afforded opportunities for sight-seeing and was generally agreed upon as a delightful interlude in the war.

We are now in camp at Scutari . . . We have a lovely view . . . which often makes me think of Switzerland. Our position is really quite lovely, and although there is an enormous barrack close by capable of holding 7000 men, I am very glad it did not fall our lot to be quartered there. It is a fine imposing building, but the filth and the stench of the rooms is beyond description and it swarms with fleas. . . . On another side is the high road to Broussa, on each side of which is the great Turkish burial-ground, extremely picturesque with its beautiful tall cypress trees and quaint tombstones topped with fezes painted – the retreat of the plaintive bulbul, which forms at night with the braying of the baggage-mules and bât-horses, the croaking of the frogs, and the howling of the scavenger dogs, the most charming soporific you can imagine (Lieutenant Colonel Frederick Stephenson, Scots Guards, May 1854).

23. Captain Burnaby, Grenadier Guards *(Fenton)*

Captain Burnaby commanded the right flank company of the
Guards during the savage hand-to-hand fighting around Sandbag Battery during the battle of Inkerman (5 November 1854).
A. W. Kinglake, drawing on eyewitness accounts, described
his part in the struggle.

*Captain Burnaby, raising his sword, laid the brave Russian dead, and
then hastening to repeat the appeal he had just before made in vain, he
cried out to his men, 'We must charge!' James Bancroft, a private
soldier of the Grenadiers, was the first to come after him, when he now
for the second time sprang up to the top of the parapet and bade his
people come on. Five or six other men of the company sprang forward
at the appeal of their captain, and Burnaby, saying to Bancroft, 'How
many will follow?' but not waiting for an answer, leapt down to the
outside of the parapet. Bancroft, following his captain, was immediately attacked by several assailants, of whom he killed one by a
bayonet-thrust in the chest; but the next instant was so grievously
wounded by a Russian bayonet tearing in through his jaw and the cage
of his teeth as to be made to stagger back a few paces before he
recommenced his exploits.*

*Captain Burnaby had but just cleared the parapet when he found
himself met by a Russian officer of great stature, who was heading the
attack at this spot, and vehemently calling forward his men. Upon
seeing Burnaby, the Russian officer sprang at him sword in hand, but
Burnaby parried; and before his assailant could again raise the arm,
brought him down by a cut so delivered on the side of the head, that the
tall leader fell, and died at once with groan. . .*

24. Royal Artillery Officers and nine-pounder cannon
(Robertson)

The artillerymen wear a variety of uniforms, either official like the undress frock coats or unofficial like the civilian jacket of the standing figure on the right. Several wear overalls with leather sewn on the inside of the legs to prevent wear whilst riding.

Unlike other officers, those of the artillery and engineers were not promoted by purchase. The 'scientific' nature of their skills meant that they underwent a course of training and were qualified by examination. By a quirk of administrative procedure, the artillery was controlled by the Board of Ordnance and not the Commander-in-Chief. This curious independence ceased in 1855 as part of the programme of army reform which followed the revelations of mismanagement during the previous winter.

25. Lieutenant Colonel Brownrigg, Grenadier Guards with two Russian boys *(Fenton)*

Tell Annie there are two Russian boys who would both like to come to England. Alma and Inkerman, such are their names; one is an orphan, the other has or had his parents in the town. They went out nutting last autumn and were taken. They cried sadly, but now would cry to go back (Roger Fenton, 29 April 1855).

26. Coldstream Guards Camp (*Robertson*)

An officer stands close to his hut. From early 1855, prefabricated huts like the one here had been sent out from England. At first they were used by officers but by the onset of the second winter, all ranks were housed in such huts. They were warmer and more comfortable than tents and long before the arrival of official consignments a handful of enterprising officers constructed their own.

5 April [1855]. *Rode into Kadekoi* [a Russian village] *and plundered an empty house of a window and a glass door. Got my hut finished, my window put in, and a good table, shelves, saddle pins & washing stands put in it. In fact I am exceedingly comfortable in it – too much so for service. All the place about it has been cleaned up. We have made a garden with flowers in it from the hills, and rock work all around* (Colonel Hodge, 4th Dragoon Guards).

27. British camp on the Sebastopol plain *(Robertson)*

High summer with soldiers in shirtsleeves and two officers (lower left) in broad brimmed 'wideawake' hats. The Crimean temperature often passed 100° in midsummer and the army had responded to the new conditions with the issue of linen trousers and coats, disparagingly nicknamed 'sandbag' coats. Coats, shirts, socks and other clothes can be seen drying on the roofs of the huts. On the right horses and mules stand in a rough earth-built paddock; presumably they represent regimental transport.

28. Officers and men of the 42nd (Royal Highland) Regiment
(Robertson)

This regiment formed part of Sir Colin Campbell's Highland Brigade. Here they wear kilts and Kilmarnock caps rather than the bonnets which they wore when they stormed the Russian position at the Alma. According to Major Ewart, of another Highland Regiment, the Scotsmen's appearance unnerved the Russians:

A Russian general, who was taken prisoner, stated that their infantry would not stand firm after they caught sight of the bare legs and waving plumes of the Highlanders (Major John Ewart, 93rd (Sutherland Highlanders) Regiment).

29. Regimental Band *(Robertson)*

A relaxed occasion in which a group of officers, many with their dogs, listened to a band and one, on the left, sits on a barrel and reads a book. The bandsmen, in their distinctive white jackets, and the officers may be from the Grenadier Guards to judge from the badges on their caps. Bandsmens' other duties included carrying the wounded from the battlefield and tending the sick.

On Saturday there was a man of the 77th [East Middlesex Regiment] *hanged for murder. I did not go, not being required to do so. It was a very extraordinary sight. The man was marched up to the gallows, the band playing the Dead March, his grave was before him. He never moved or changed countenance and did not appear to be at all concerned. There were a certain number of men from each Regt. present. The sight must have been most imposing and very rare; this is the first execution that has taken place here* (Lieutenant Robert Campbell, 71st Regiment (Highland Light Infantry), 25 February 1856).

30. Regimental Lines *(Robertson)*

These tents are very comfortable things in dry weather, but most uncomfortable in wet weather, where so many are crowded into one tent. First of all your head must not touch it. Then your comrades coming in wet, tired and covered with mud — you get a good share of wet and mud from them if you are not in the same state yourself, so that it is continually uncomfortable. If you sit down it must be in a doubled up position with your head nearly touching your knees. If you lie down you get kicked and trod on by all comers. Still, these tents sheltered us from the severer elements (Corporal Fisher, 95th Rifles).

31. Officers of 18th Regiment (Royal Irish Rangers), May 1856
(Robertson)

This picture shows a party and was presented by James Robertson to his friend, the chef Alexis Soyer. Plenty of drink seems available and one figure, framed in the window and wearing a fez, is having his tankard filled. Two dogs, one lying by the reclining officer on the right and the other on the lap of the seated figure below the window, complete the scene. Colonel Edwards, the regiment's commanding officer, is seated on the right with his cap on his knee. A veteran of the first Opium and Burma wars, he was a stern disciplinarian.

Our old colonel was a very proud man and he would glory in seeing a man flogged, especially if he thought he was a bit stubborn and while the flogging was going on he would growl and grumble at the flogger for not hitting harder (Private Daniel Bourke, 18th Regiment).

32. Colonel Tinley and officers, 39th (Dorsetshire) Regiment
(*Fenton*)

[23 April 1855] *There is a photographic picture taken out here – we had a group of some of our fellows taken I on my horse, when they are struck off I will send you one.*
[30 April] *I send you a fancy portrait of yr. affectionate son – I am afraid you will not recognize his well known features but still it may give you some idea – Everybody is having their picture taken in the photographic style – My horse which is a very handsome one looks like a mule and Col. Tinley's is not much better . . . Maunsell* [killed in action 18 July 1855] *is the man with the black beard and Dekolech is next to him with the grenade in his cap – Ogilvy is the man on the right* [left in the photograph]*, his regiment is in India and he came out as an amateur to see the fun* (Lieutenant Charles Milligan, 39th Foot, the mounted figure on the left).

33. Lieutenant General Sir Robert Garrett (1794–1869) and officers of the 46th (South Devonshire) Regiment *(Fenton)*

General Garrett, who had been commissioned in 1811 and saw service in the Peninsula, is the second figure from the left. Very much a hard and hardened soldier of the old school, he had been in command of the 46th at the outbreak of the war when the regiment was undertaking garrison duties at Windsor. From this time dated the public scandal which had earned Garrett and his regiment much public and press opprobrium. A court martial had revealed a series of brutal incidents within the officers' mess where loutishness, foul language and 'deep gambling' were the rule. The victim of much of the spiteful bullying which characterized the officers was a Lieutenant Parry, the son of a tradesman. Garrett cared little about this and seems to have made no effort to intervene. For *Punch*, he was a

> *fine old English Colonel who sits up rather late*
> *And drinks his grog while at the door bullied Lieutenants wait.*

34. General Sir Robert Garrett with officers of the 46th South Devonshire Regiment *(Fenton)*

The general is seated on the right and is having either lunch or dinner.

I am very tired of my salt pork. It is generally so fat that I can hardly eat it, and I shall be very glad when the boxes sent from home make their appearance. It was most kind of my Mother to think of sending them, and the articles enumerated in the list are exactly those which are most appreciated out here.

. . . Portable soup. Lyons Sausages
Piece of Bacon (Strasbourg)
2 tins of Chocolate Powder
Salt, Pepper, Ginger, Peppermint
2 tins concentrated Cream
2lb Bologna Sausages
A case fine Brandy. Three Flasks of ditto. Tea, Wine, Cheese

(Lieutenant John Campbell, 71st Regiment (Highland Light Infantry), 23 March 1855)

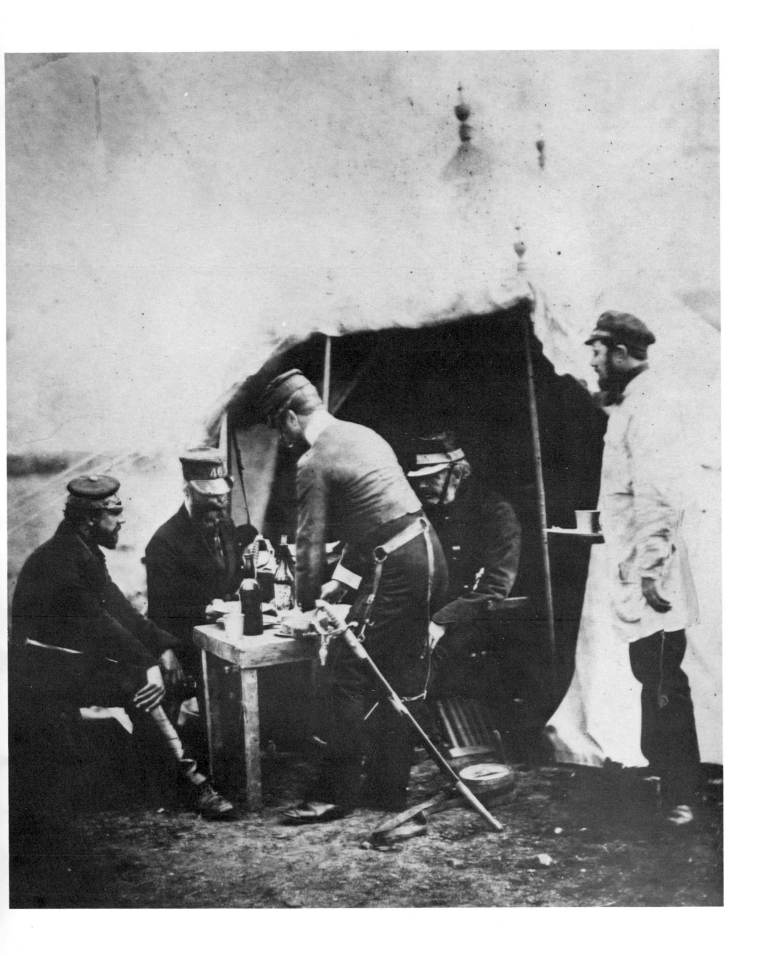

35. Colonel Wood, Major Stuart Wortley and Colonel the Hon. F. Colborne *(Fenton)*

The hut looks like a local building with a turf roof to which has been added a door, probably made of packing cases, and a window for which some glass has been found. A telescope case hangs over the door and beside Colonel Wood, an artillery officer, is his dogs. Many dogs accompanied their owners to the campaign and others, pariahs from Balaklava, were adopted by officers and men. They often served a useful purpose:

When we arrived in camp, the tents were struck and our comrades were quite busy rat hunting – they seemed to have taken a particular liking to our tents. Under the boards we found as many as three nests of them and men and dogs had to do the office of ratcatchers. We had a favourite dog belonging to the Regt. whose name was 'Soldier' and who was a capital dog at rat killing as well as soldiering. He endured all the hardships of the fore part of the Campaign without a wine [sic] and continued to do his duty to the last when one day it appeared that an officer of some other Reg. owed him a grudge for worrying his dog, and gave him a slashing with his sword which caused his death (Corporal Fisher, 95th Rifles).

36. 57th (West Middlesex) Regiment *(Fenton)*

The regiment is drawn up in companies. The furled colours are in the centre and on the left are two drummers. Together with the 38th (**37**) the 57th made up one of the columns which took part in the unsuccessful assault on the Redan (**63**) on 18 June 1855. Whilst crossing over 400 yards of open ground, the regiment came under heavy fire from Russian cannon and muskets. It lost its colonel and 113 casualties out of 400 men. These losses and the failure of the attack were ascribed to inadequate planning.

The men, I understand, did not behave well. But this, no doubt arose from mismanagement of the attack [i.e. Raglan's plan] *and is possibly a good lesson for some of our officers, who always think that British pluck has done and can do, everything. Now British pluck is not absolutely universal. When present it is as good as any pluck, and in some respects better but without head is worth very little* (Colonel C. A. Windham, 20 June 1855).

37. Lieutenant General Sir John Campbell with the Light Company of the 38th (South Staffordshire) Regiment *(Fenton)*

General Campbell, who stands apart and to the left, commanded the 4th Division (made up of the 38th and 57th regiments) in the attack on the Redan. 'A good tempered and agreeable man', Campbell insisted on leading the assault troops in person.

General Bentinck gave strict orders to Sir John not to lead the storming party, and I too begged him to turn his attention more to direction, and less to leading; but I saw it was of no use, and told Hume, his A.D.C., that I was sure he would make a rush, which was exactly what he did, and accordingly lost his life, and did not win. Poor fellow, he was as kind-hearted and gallant a man as you would meet anywhere but, alas for his wife and family, he thought of nothing but carrying the Redan with his own sword (Colonel C. A. Windham).

38. The Reverend Henry Wright, principal chaplain to the forces in the Crimea with other chaplains *(Fenton)*

At the time of the outbreak of war, there were only seven chaplains for the whole British army since the reduction in their numbers had been regarded as a justifiable economy by the Horse Guards. A few dedicated officers attempted to cater for the spiritual welfare of their men through prayer meetings and Bible study sessions, but such enthusiasm was unpopular in many messes. After the war the number of chaplains was increased to twenty-two and Roman Catholics and Presbyterians were included for the first time. At the hospital at Scutari, near Constantinople, the religious life of the troops received greater attention, if only as a means to reduce drunkenness among the convalescents.

. . . no sooner was a poor soldier discharged from the Hospital ward as convalescent, than ten to one, he was returned in a few hours almost dead from the effects of drink . . . Now the case was different, and the soldiers gladly availed themselves of the entertaining and instructive lectures which were provided for them.

One of these lectures must have special mention. It was given by a chaplain, the Rev. Mr Connors, who took much interest in the men, and was always anxious to promote their welfare. Mr Connor's (sic) was on birds, which was very interesting and exceedingly well sustained, and ended with a remarkable graceful allusion to a certain sweet songster, 'whose notes were not confined to England's woods and forests, but were the solace of the sick chamber, the soother of the sorrowful, the harbinger of ease to the wounded, and the notes of a friend to the soldier. I need not name that bird,' said Mr Connors, whereupon the building seemed ready to fall from the burst of applause and cheering, as every voice vociferated 'The Nightingale, the Nightingale'. (Lady Alicia Blackwood).

39. Paymaster Henry Duberly (8th Hussars) and Mrs Duberly
(Fenton)

Mrs Duberly published an account of her experiences in the Crimea in 1855 (*Journal kept during the Russian War*). She was one of the handful of wives who were permitted to follow their husbands during the campaign; her presence and her interests were considered distasteful in some quarters.

You ask me if I know Mrs Duberly, I do by sight very well, and should like to see her book, though I would not give a pin for her opinions. She is known in the camp by the name of the Vulture, from the pleasure she seemed to take in riding over fields of battle. I should think her feelings (if she has any) cannot be very fine, and she is certainly more fit to follow a camp then to live in an English drawing room (Captain Temple Godman, 5th Dragoon Guards, 17 March 1856).

[Mrs Duberly] is an odd woman. The French have dedicated a Polka to her, as 'The Amazone'. I do not believe she is guilty of that which many say she is, but of course she has many 'Followers' as the servant girls say, and her vanity causes her to encourage them (Lieutenant-Colonel Forrest, 4th Dragoon Guards quoted by Colonel Hodge).

The grass is plain and beautiful. Mr & Mrs Duberly and Paulet Somerset [Lord Raglan's nephew and A.D.C. see **42.**] *out grazing. The publicity of all this is very disgusting* (Colonel Hodge, 4th Dragoon Guards, 9 May 1855).

40. Soldiers of the 86th (Royal County Down) Regiment skirmishing *(Captain H. R. S. Chatfield)*

The conditions of battle made it impossible for Crimean photographers to show troops in action. This posed photograph of about 1865 gives a good impression of a company of British troops skirmishing; figures are seen loading and firing Enfield muzzle-loading rifles and an officer directs their movement. This photograph is one from a private album compiled by an officer of the 86th and was presumably taken during exercises.

3. Britain's Allies

41. Marshal Aimable Jean-Jacques Pélissier *(Fenton)*

Pélissier took command of the French forces in the Crimea on 19 May 1855 and later directed the attacks on the Malakov fort. An able soldier but a rough Norman in his manners, he drew some sharp remarks from British officers. Captain Godman described him as *'a very fat, coarse, vulgar looking man, more like an old coalheaver than a General, however he is one of the right sort'*. Fenton dined with him and came away with mixed impressions:

General Pélissier kept all the conversation to himself, and his conversation is not brilliant. He is a very good personification of the French army, for he is rough in his manners, though not without a certain bonhomie. *He cares nothing for the sacrifice of life, and does not seem troubled with scruples of any kind. His face has the expression of brutal boldness something like that of a wild boar. However, he is coming tomorrow* [7 June 1855] *to have his likeness taken: I mean to have a good one of him* (Roger Fenton).

42. British and French staff officers at Headquarters *(Fenton)*

On the extreme right is Lieutenant Colonel Vico, the French commissioner at British Headquarters. From September 1854 until his death from cholera in July 1855, he was the principal liaison officer between the two armies. Seated and holding a light-coloured cane is Mr Calvert, head of the British Army's intelligence service and one of the very few men on the staff who could speak Russian. He too died in July 1855 of cholera.

Mr Calvert also had rendered many important services. He had formed a corps of guides, consisting mostly of Tartar chiefs, and had established communications with the principal towns in the Crimea. Much valuable information was obtained through his judicious arrangements, and latterly no body of troops of the enemy's army could move, or even shift their camps, without intelligence of the fact being immediately transmitted to the English Headquarters. His loss was one not easily replaced (Colonel S. J. C. Calthorpe, Headquarters Staff).

The right hand figure, seated on the steps is probably Colonel Paulet Somerset, Raglan's A.D.C. (see **39**)

43. General Bosquet with A.D.Cs *(Fenton)*

General Bosquet commanded the 2nd *Corps D'Armée* at Alma and Inkerman. Later he found himself at loggerheads with Pélissier and briefly resigned his command in protest against his senior's plans for the attack on Sebastopol. The staff officer on the far right wears the uniform of a Zouave officer and has a fine pointed 'Imperial', a beard grown by many French officers in imitation of their Emperor, Napoleon III.

General Bosquet is a very good take resembling much the portrait of Napoleon when he began to grow stout, only there is an expression of frankness and good temper which does not exist in Napoleon's portrait. He has promised me horses to convey my van, and all that I need while staying with him. His staff are very nice fellows (Roger Fenton).

44. Mounted French infantry officer *(Fenton)*

The courage of the French army earned widespread admiration among the English and their organization provoked envy and regret.

Since then [the time of the Peninsular War] *we have for more than a generation applied ourselves to the arts of peace, to the entire neglect of military science; and it has now become our turn to learn from the French* (Sir Charles Trevelyan, Assistant Secretary to the Treasury, May 1855).

[The French] *are fine looking men, a great many of them are much taller than I am (six feet), and if they get a chance, will most likely make their mark on the Russians* (Sergeant Gowing, Royal Fusiliers).

45. Officer and troopers of the Chasseurs d'Afrique *(Fenton)*

Among the best French cavalry, the Chasseurs wore a dashing uniform. The cap was red as were the baggy overalls and the jackets were pale blue. The officer's uniform is decorated with lace and he wears the smaller *kepi* which continued in use until the First World War.

The Chasseurs charged in support of the Light Brigade at Balaklava and silenced one Russian battery.

The gallant conduct of the Chasseurs d'Afrique deserves especial mention. Formed on the left of the light cavalry, as the latter advanced to the charge, the Chasseurs rushed upon the artillery of the enemy stationed on the Fedhukine heights, turned their flank, and put their gunners to the sword; thus making an important diversion in which they suffered rather severely (Major Adye, R.A).

46. French Zouaves *(Fenton)*

The zouaves were originally native troops from Algeria but by the time of the Crimean War their ranks were almost entirely European although their uniform was distinctly North African in appearance. For zeal, bravery and often rashness, they were unequalled. Their pluck and independence delighted the British.

. . . certainly the finest troops for courage after the English (Captain Portal, 4th Light Dragoons).

We hear that the Zouaves fought like so many tigers, and although the odds were heavy against them, they routed the enemy off the field. I don't think I ever told you before that they are not all Frenchmen that wear French uniforms. The Zouaves have a number of English and Irish mixed up with them – wild spirits that join them on account of rapid promotion (Sergeant Gowing, Royal Fusiliers).

47. French Cantinière *(Fenton)*

Cantinières were attached to every French regiment. They were often the wives of N.C.O.s and they managed canteens as well as selling additional rations. Each carried a small barrel of brandy from which they sold tots to the troops. Their dress followed closely that of their regiment. This cantinière was attached to a zouave regiment and therefore wore baggy trousers beneath her broad-skirted coat.

48. French artillery battery *(Robertson)*

The bombardment opened on the left front and the Russians answered the French fire which was splendid (about 400 guns) with great vigour from about 350 guns, much to the astonishment of the French who expected to have it all their own way, and who were so much taken by surprise, that at one time it was a very doubtful thing which of the two, French or Russians, would beat down the other's fire. The Russians fortunately gave in time to save the French, who could not hold out much longer, and since then the Russians have fired very little on the left, whereas the French open all at once, about 4 or 5 times a day, every gun they have at the same instant, and keep it up for an hour or so without intermission. It is awful and splendid to see the French open on the left in this way, they make the Russians batteries dance with shot and shell (Major Henry Clifford, 77th (East Middlesex) Regiment, 7 September 1855).

49. Omar Pasha (1806–1871) *(Fenton)*

A Croatian Moslem convert, Omar had defeated the Russians in Silistria in 1854 and later took command of the Turkish forces before Sebastopol.

He is a capital fellow. Quite different to the Turks in general, hates all display . . . He is a sporting looking fellow and sits well on his horse in a plain grey frock coat and long jack boots, he is very fond of horses (Captain Nigel Kingscote, A.D.C. to Lord Raglan).

50. Colonel Arthur Cunynghame, orderly, and Ensign Arthur Ellis, 33rd (Duke of Wellington's, West Riding) Regiment
(Fenton)

In May 1855, shortly after this picture was taken, Colonel Cunynghame was seconded to the Turkish army with the rank of Lieutenant General. Several British officers were given commands in the Turkish forces of whom 20,000 were receiving British pay by 1855. In October 1855, Cunynghame took charge of a force of 10,000 Turks which occupied Kertch (on the eastern seaboard of the Crimea) for the winter. He is the figure standing in the centre. Ensign Ellis appears to have been his A.D.C. and was remembered by Major Ewart of the 93rd as a 'charming lad' after a dinner party with Cunynghame.

51. Ismail Pasha with Turkish soldiers *(Fenton)*

These Turkish soldiers fraternize immensely, a party of privates came the other day into one of our tents where a party of us were sitting talking and began inspecting and admiring everything. They were particularly delighted with an air bed and a revolver we showed them, the odd thing is that they and apparently all troops but the English behave quite like gentlemen sitting down and talking perfectly at their ease and lighting a pipe and sticking it between our lips with the most courtly air in the world (Captain Cuninghame, 95th Rifles, 19 August 1854).

Sadly, the more common attitude was one of callous xenophobia and brutal contempt:

The Johnnys [Turks] *are made to do all the dirty work, that is as much as the idle rascals can be forced to do. Everyone pushes and cuffs them, especially the sailors, who make great fuss of them. They work now in the trenches and when Jack* [i.e., Jack Tar] *sees a shell coming, he picks up a stone which he lets drive at Johnny, just as the shell bursts somewhere near, who feeling himself hit drops his spade, and runs about howling, to the immense delight of Jack and his comrades* (Captain Godman, 5th Dragoon Guards, 17 December 1854).

52. Bashi-Bazouk and companion *(Szathmari)*

Mounted, irregular troops, the Bashi-Bazouks were used by the Turkish army in the Silistrian campaign in the spring of 1854 when this photograph was taken. Their demeanour and appearance did not impress the British.

About 4000 Bashi Bazooks passed through our camp at Aladyn, on their way towards Varna, from Shumla; they were wild-looking fellows, each man dressed and armed according to his own fancy. Some had long lances, and all two or three pistols and a knife, besides a sword, whilst several carried a flag. The horses were all small but seemed active . . .
About this time General Yussuf, of the French army, and Colonel Beatson, were appointed to command two divisions of Bashi Bazooks, who were sadly in want of instruction in drill and discipline (Major Ewart, 93rd Regiment [Sutherland Highlanders], June 1854).

53. Turkish Irregulars *(Fenton)*

I had no sooner pitched my tent than quite a mob of Turks appeared at the door. I asked a sergeant what it was all about. 'Oh,' he said, 'send them away, I never listen to them; send them away.' I replied, 'Is there not an interpreter? Please find him.' Then a shabby little Greek shuffled up and made a polite bow, and I proceeded to hear what the Turks had to say. The first man that came up began to speak and gesticulate wildly. 'Oh,' said the interpreter,' that's a man that speaks a language no one understands, not even the Turks; but he makes energetic signs, which, I believe, mean that he wants to go home, as he is always pointings towards the south.' Poor fellow! I wonder where the Turks caught him, but of course we shall never know. I had him shipped off with a good bag of sovereigns tied round his waist, as they were actually due to him as pay, and it was then that I got from the Turks themselves, through the interpreter, how they had enlisted. They came from a variety of districts in the Turkish empire (Acting Major J. P. Robertson, 31st [Huntingdonshire] Regiment).

54. Austrian infantry and cavalry officers at Bucharest (*Viktor von Angerer*)

Austrian forces occupied Moldavia and Wallachia in 1854 after the Russian withdrawal and the threat that Austria, already allied with the British and French, would intervene actively in the war helped to persuade the Russians to negotiate in the winter of 1855–6. This photograph shows Austrian officers, possibly of the General Staff. In the foreground, just to the right of the white-coated officer is a figure in a dark uniform who is possibly a Russian officer.

4. Weapons

55. Private soldiers and officers of the 3rd Regiment (The Buffs) piling arms *(Fenton)*

Nearly all the British forces which landed in the Crimea in 1854 were armed with the Minié rifle which had recently been adopted, following advice given by Wellington shortly before his death. The Minié was a muzzle-loading rifle with a range of up to 1,000 yards and was in every way superior to the Russian muskets. In pitched battles the British were always at an advantage thanks to the fire-power of the Minié. The soldiers here are in various forms of battle dress; the figure on the left wears the Kilmarnock cap and overcoat and those in the centre, the 'Albert' Shako with scarlet coatee.

56. Royal Marine artillery officers *(Robertson)*

Royal Marine artillery, alongside guns manned by sailors and regular artillerymen, formed the British batteries which shelled the defences and town of Sebastopol. The gun positions were frequently mauled by Russian sallies and the gunners had to defend themselves. The officer in the centre carries a revolver. The Colt and Adams revolvers used by many officers and N.C.Os. were not issued by the army and had to be purchased independently. They were five or six shot percussion revolvers and soon proved their value in hand-to-hand fighting. During the Charge of the Heavy Brigade, Cornet Handley, having been stabbed by four cossacks, was able to shoot three with his revolver.

57. Siege Battery *(Robertson)*

For the greater part, the fighting in the Crimea consisted of bombardments and counter-bombardments, duels between the Allied and the Russian artillery. The Allied purpose was to 'soften up' the Russian defences, prior to an assault, and the Russians were determined to force the Allies from their trenches and gun positions. The guns are mounted behind earthworks and behind them are bunkers of earth and stone in which the crews could shelter during bombardment. Other defences seen in the photograph are gabions, wicker baskets filled with earth and stones, which were widely used alongside the more familiar sandbags (see **48**). In the distance, beyond the battery is open ground with Sebastopol and the sea beyond. Amongst the debris in the foreground are a number of spent Russian cannon balls.

Last night when I was in the trenches I saw one of the most magnificent shelling matches that has taken place during the siege at least. All of a sudden without apparently any particular reason, every available gun and mortar in Sebastopol seem to have been discharged at the French right, all loaded with shell and some with 13 or 16 small ones. The shells which are easily seen by night crossing each other in every direction and bursting one after the other, some in the air and some on the ground, produced a more splendid firework display than I ever saw before. I am sure there must have been 100 shells in the air at once; the Russians have a nasty trick of loading one big mortar with a number of small shells generally 16 in number, these spread in every direction and must be extremely inconvenient to those against whom they are directed, fortunately for us they reserve these delicate little attentions for the French (Captain Cuninghame, 95th Rifles).

58. The 21 Gun Naval Battery *(Robertson)*

It was in these siege works that the strength of the Russians was worn down, until they withdrew across the harbour – the battles, glorious as they were, being merely incidents in the struggle.

. . . Two guns in the Redan (see **64**) *enfiladed the left-hand guns of the right (or eastern) face of the 21-gun battery, and as I passed them a shell close over my head made me stoop, till I felt my foot on something soft, and a hasty step repeated the sensation. Looking down, I saw I was treading on the stomachs of two dead men, who had been fighting their guns stripped to the waist when killed, and whose bodies had been placed together. I was not only startled but shocked, and the feeling made me hold my head up when in danger for the next eight months* (Mid-Shipman Evelyn Wood, R.N.).

59. Nine-pounder gun and team, Royal Artillery *(Robertson)*

On several occasions at the Alma and Inkerman, the well-served British guns found themselves out-ranged and out shot by the heavier Russian batteries. Nevertheless, at both battles, they played a crucial role, particularly at Inkerman where 18-pound cannon were dragged up from the siege park and used to drive Russian artillery from the field.

The Royal Artillery deserve the greatest credit for the part they played at the battle of Inkerman, as the Russian guns were much more numerous, and most of them of heavier calibre, than those of the British. Altogether there were thirty-six British field-guns (9-pounder guns and 24-pounder howitzers), besides the two 18-pounders; the French brought into action eighteen of their guns; so that the allies had just fifty-six guns, opposed to ninety-four Russian ones — fifty-four of the latter being 12-pounder and 32-pounder howitzers (Major Ewart, 93rd [Sutherland Highlanders] Regiment).

5. Fields of Battle

60. Sebastopol *(Robertson)*

This panoramic photograph was taken from the slopes just below the Malakov fort (**65**) and shows clearly how that strongpoint overlooked the town. The Russians abandoned the town on the night of 8–9 September 1855, after the French had captured the Malakov. The following day, jubilant and curious Allied soldiers poured into the town to look and pillage.

Directly after breakfast yesterday I set out to see what I could. No one was allowed to enter the town through our lines except with a pass, but Colonel Barker got me in as his adjutant and we set out on a voyage of discovery. We first went to the cemetery and so on to the Arsenal, to the left of the Dockyard Creek; we went on to the Club, where we found the wine running out of the doors and crowds of tipsy Frenchmen . . . (Lieutenant Robert Biddulph, R.A., 10 September 1855).

The horrors inside the town, where the enemy had established their hospitals, baffle all description. Some of our non-commissioned officers and men went into those places and described scenes as heart-rending and revolting in the extreme. Many of the buildings were full of dead and dying mutilated bodies, without anyone to give them a drink of water. Poor fellows, they had well defended their country's cause and were now left to die in agony, unattended, uncared for, packed as closely as they could be stowed away, saturated in blood, and with the crash of exploding forts all around them. They had served the Tsar but too well; there they lay, in a state of nudity, literally rolling in their blood.

Our officers and men, both French and English found their way there indiscriminately, and at once set to work to relieve them. Medical aid was brought as quickly as possible to them, but hundreds passed beyond all earthly appearance (Sergeant Gowing, Royal Fusiliers).

61. Sebastopol Dockyard before demolition *(Robertson)*

The Russian naval dockyards were destroyed by the Royal Engineers in November 1855. They had been the reason why the Allies were determined to capture Sebastopol and their demolition, in British eyes, meant the removal of any threat from the Russian navy in the Black and Mediterranean Seas.

62. Sebastopol dockyard after demolition *(Robertson)*

I took a most interesting walk yesterday over the Mamelon, the Malakoff, and the Karalbelnaya suburb including the celebrated docks, which are extremely fine work. It is, however, being mined in all directions, and the mines will not be completed for another month, although the sappers are working at them every day. I should think that at the end of that time they will explode them. It seems rather barbarous at first sight to destroy such beautiful works, which must have cost millions to construct, but considering that they formed part of a gigantic plan for conquest, and never can be used for any legitimate purpose, it would be folly to leave them untouched (Lieutenant Colonel Stephenson, Scots Guards, 20 October 1855).

63. Glacis of the Redan *(Robertson)*

Together with the Malakov (**65**), the Redan formed the
strongest point among the outer defences of Sebastopol. This
was well understood by the Russians who had, under the
instruction of Colonel Todleben, shown enormous energy and
ingenuity in fortifying both strongpoints. The Allies realized
that they were the key to Sebastopol and encouraged by the
growing numbers of men and equipment available, Marshal
Pélissier forcefully urged a determined attack on the Redan and
Malakov in the summer. Raglan agreed, and on 6 June 1855 the
preliminary bombardment began. On 18 June (the fortieth
anniversary of Waterloo) the British attacked the Redan and the
French attempted the Malakov. Both attacks were beaten back
with heavy losses.

*Still on we went, staggering beneath the terrible hail. Our Colonel fell
dead, our Adjutant the same, and almost every officer we had with us
fell dead or wounded; but still we pressed on until we were stopped by
the chevaux de frise, and in front of that our poor fellows lay in piles.
We were met with a perfect hell of fire, at about fifty yards from us, of
grape, shot, shell, canister, and musketry, and could not return a shot.*

*The enemy mounted the parapets of the Redan and delivered volley
after volley into us. They hoisted a large black flag and defied us to
come on* (Sergeant Gowing, Royal Fusiliers).

64. The Redan interior *(Robertson)*

At the beginning of September 1855, the Allies prepared for a second assault on the Redan and Malakov. On 5 September over 800 guns opened a three-day bombardment in which 90,000 rounds of round shot and 13,000 shells were thrown against the Russian positions. The assaults were launched on the 8th when, as before, the British were forced to endure a savage fire. The Redan was finally taken and briefly held before the depleted British were forced out by a Russian counter-attack.

Robertson's photograph shows how the defences had been pummelled by artillery fire and the Russian's own efforts at demolition, made before their withdrawal. When Captain Godman visited the abandoned fort, the debris of battle and death were still present.

*I then went to the Redan, and it seems to me we should never have attacked it, for it is quite commanded by the Malakoff (see **65**), and could not be held when we were in, but the French said we must go at it to draw off the men from other parts. The Russians were there in heaps, and the ditch was nearly full of dead English piled one on the other, I suppose five feet thick or more. The Redan was terribly strong, and bombproof inside. There was not a place an inch large that was not ploughed up by our shot and shell, guns, gabions; and even pieces of human flesh of every shape and size were scattered about, it was absolutely torn to pieces, and one mass of rubbish and confusion impossible to describe* (Captain Godman, 5th Dragoon Guards, 10 September 1855).

65. French trenches facing the Malakov *(Robertson)*

When, on 8 September 1855, the tricolour was raised over the Malakov and the fort was in French hands, the Russians were left with no choice but to abandon the Redan (**64**) and Sebastopol itself. In effect, the war had ended although the peace treaty was not signed until the following spring.

The photograph shows the French trenches with their gabions, fascines (bundles of long sticks laid horizontally) and sandbags. The trenches in foreground shelter a battery of howitzers and those beyond and leading up to the Malakov are the zig-zag sap trenches by which the French approached for the final assault.

66. Trenches near Inkerman looking towards Sebastopol
(Robertson)

Much of the life of the Allied armies centred around the trenches to the south and east of Sebastopol. Here were the batteries for bombardment and frequently the scenes of fighting when the Russians made sorties from their lines. Shipping can just be seen lying in the approaches to Sebastopol harbour, over the ridges in the centre of the photograph. The top grey line is the sea-sky horizon.

When we beat off the Russians the first time, I went to post a few sentries in front whilst Buochier carried away his wounded. Hardly had we advanced 20 yards when pop, whiz, whiz, pop went the Russians about 30 yards in front. My party at once bolted, but by shrieking at them like a maniac I made them lie down and fire. My appearance close to them with a sword in one hand and a pistol in the other being, I suppose, more formidable than the Russians farther off. We have completely taken the shine out of the whole Army now, even the red soldiers (Cuninghame's regiment wore dark green jackets) *themselves allow it. All the field officers who command in the trenches say that the only troops they can rely on for the front are our men. The worst of that is that from being always in advance our men get no sleep in the trenches, which is very hard lines, as at the best they only get 1 night out of 2 in bed. We, the officers, are better off, getting 2 out of every 3* (Captain Cuninghame, 95th Rifles, 27 November 1854).

Sometimes we would dig and guard in turn; we could keep ourselves warm, digging and making the trenches and batteries, although often up to our ankles in muddy water. As for the covering party, it was killing work laying down for hours in the cold mud, returning to the camp at daylight, wearied completely out with cold, sleepy and hungry – many a poor fellow suffering with ague or fever, to find nothing but a cold bleak mud tent, without fire, to rest their bones in (Sergeant Gowing, Royal Fusiliers).

67. The battlefield at Inkerman *(Robertson)*

This photograph looks south east, across the Tchernaya river, to the heights of Inkerman. On 5 November 1854, in drizzle and fog, 60,000 Russian troops launched an offensive against British positions. This picture shows the northern sector of the battlefield where the Russians unsuccessfully attempted to dislodge British forces occupying the ridge in the middle distance. In the middle of this ridge beyond the quarry was the Sandbag Battery which was fiercely contested and the scene of a grim hand-to-hand struggle (**23**). Eventually, with French reinforcements, the British sent the Russians back with heavy casualties.

68. 'Valley of Death' *(Robertson)*

This view, which when it was first reproduced was given the
title 'Valley of Death', was not the scene of the Light Brigade's
charge, but a ravine, possibly close to the battlefield at Inkerman and certainly within range of the Russian artillery, as
evidenced by the number of spent cannonballs lying on the
ground. On the hillside is a sandbagged position; the whole
gives a good, close impression of the upland around Sebastopol.

69. The battlefield of Tchernaya *(Robertson)*

This picture shows the Tractir bridge over the River Tchernaya; in the foreground is the aqueduct which carried water to the docks at Sebastopol. On 16 August 1855, a Russian army of 57,000 under General Gorchakov launched an attack on French and Sardinian troops on the Fedioukine Heights (from whose lower slopes this picture was taken). This ill-judged Russian assault was beaten off with heavy losses after hand-to-hand fighting on the ground around and beyond the bridge.

The fight was short but sharp . . . I rode over the ground just after; it is a terrible sight when the excitement is over to see men torn in messes by round shot and shell, and then the wounded moaning and dying all round. If kings' ministers could see a few such sights I think countries would not be hurried into war (Captain Godman, 5th Dragoon Guards, 17 August 1855).

6. Supplies

70. Balaklava Harbour *(Robertson)*

Balaklava harbour was the lifeline of the British army, the conduit through which flowed all the weapons, ammunition, supplies, food and animals required for its existence. In the early months of the siege conditions were chaotic and organization was ramshackle.

No storehouses were established at Balaklava, though plenty of houses for the purpose might have been found. Stores were kept on board ship, where they could not be readily got at, or found, and troops were often in want of things which were secreted carelessly in the holds of vessels in the harbour.

I was told by an officer in command of one of the beautiful merchant steamers, which had done so much for us, that he found the greatest difficulty in getting rid of his cargo, though he well knew how much needed the items were. He had a most miscellaneous cargo. Horseshoes, sixpences and ball cartridges (Lieutenant Colonel George Evelyn, attached to the Turkish army, 13 January 1855).

71. Shipping in Balaklava harbour *(Robertson)*

By the spring of 1855, the Sanitary Commission appointed to
improve the conditions at Balaklava had got its work in hand.
A cleansing staff was organized, latrines were erected, drains
were made, Naval Surgeons daily inspected the ships, dead
animals were towed out to sea and temporary quays were built
over the accumulated rubbish. 'As healthy a little seaport as
can be seen' was the congratulatory conclusion of the Commissioner's report.

72. Railway stores on the quayside at Balaklava *(Fenton)*

Our railway had made rapid progress. Already it has passed a little village called Kadikoi, outside this town (Balaklava) *about a mile and a half, and is close to the Cavalry camp. That portion of the line is now in use, and stores and wooden huts etc. are being carried up in large quantities by it: the large railway carts being dragged along the line by some gigantic English carthorses* (Staff Assistant Surgeon Lawson, 25 February 1855).

73. Cattle and carts leaving Balaklava harbour (*Fenton*)

By the time that this picture was taken (March 1855), the rudiments of a transport corps were in being although their advent did not end the traditional arrangements for moving supplies.

'Is Sergeant Gowing in?' 'Yes; what's up?' 'You are for fatigue at once'. Off to Balaklava, perhaps to bring up supplies, in the shape of salt beef, salt pork, biscuits, blankets, shot and shell. Return at night completely done-up; down you go in the mud for a few hours' rest – that is if there is not an alarm. And thus it continued, week in and week out, month in and month out (Sergeant Gowing, Royal Fusiliers).

74. Unloading stores at Balaklava *(Fenton)*

Matters are certainly improving rapidly here, the men have all got sheep-skin coats which are splendid warm things. They almost always get full rations. The Duke of Wellington has made our Regiment a most handsome present of 30 doz. capital brandy to each battalion for the Officers; Prince Albert has also sent out 20 game pies and 20 tins of venison soup to each Battn. as well as 2 tons of the best Cavendish tobacco for the men of our 2 Battns., the 3 Regiments of Guards and the 11th Huzzars. Everyone seems vying with each other in the endeavour to do something for us. A public spirited individual (whose name I don't know) has sent out 60 tins of liquid coffee for the party who took the Rifle Pits (Captain Cuninghame 95th Rifles, 2 February 1855).

75. Merchant seaman on dromedary *(Fenton)*

This was one of the animals purchased in the Middle East along with horses and mules which replaced losses in the winter of 1854–5 and formed the basis for a transport corps capable of meeting the demands of the war. Few dromedaries seem to have been used and there is little evidence to suggest whether they were of value, beyond the provision, as in this case, of entertainment.

76. Balaklava harbour *(Robertson)*

The tower above the harbour is part of a Genoese fort, below and to the left are the huts of the hospital.

'As to Balaklava harbour,' wrote our friend, 'it is most extraordinary, a wonder of the world; its narrow entrance, its high rocky sides, deep waters, and beautiful anchorage for ships. I have never seen anything which has struck me so powerfully for a monument of British power, energy and wealth, as the appearance of things in Balaklava and the camp. It seems as if a part of England has been transported bodily to the Crimea. No picture conveys an idea of it. The railway running along to the harbour with its locomotives, and a capital military road running for miles in several directions is now covered with strings of mules and waggons. Warehouses, shops, cafes – English, French, and Greek – are crowded with customers, and the whole place is alive like a series of populous towns in the industrial regions of England, swarming with people full of energy and work, beyond the ordinary energy of peace at home.' (Lady Alicia Blackwood).

77. Kamiesch harbour *(Robertson)*

I took a beautiful ride to Kamiesch Bay, about 9 miles from Balaklava. I was greatly and agreeably surprised with my visit. Kamiesch is to the French, what Balaklava is to the English. It is the harbour to which all the vessels for French come in and discharge their cargo. Unlike Balaklava the neighbourbood all around is rather flat, the harbour is more than four times as large, and contains about five or six times as many vessels as Balaklava. There is certainly a degree of arrangement about the place which there is not about our little town. Everything has its place, huts are stored up in large numbers, and wood in sufficient quantities for six months' consumption, and commissariat provisions in large quantities. The shops consist, as they do in our case, of a number of wooden huts, with the frontage open and arranged in a somewhat tasteful manner. They are put up so as to form streets, all of which have a name, and from the presence of respectable looking women in the streets, the place assumes a degree of civilization which is not witnessed in our Donnybrook Fair (Staff Assistant Surgeon Lawson, April 1855).

78. Kamiesch *(Robertson)*

They [the French at Kamiesch] *have erected long huts and made quite a village . . . The wounded are carefully laid on beds in rows, then come the sick and so on; everything clean and nice; the man's name and complaint on a piece of paper over his bed, as if he was in a barrack hospital. Then they have huts in which all the medicines are arranged and everything got at, at a moment's notice. Then again, close to the hospital huts, are large cooking huts where soup is constantly made* (Captain Portal, 4th Light Dragoons).

7. The Royal Navy

79. H.M.S. St George *(Anonymous)*

The Crimean War was the last occasion when wooden-built, sail-driven British battleships went into action, looking much as they did in Nelson's day. This ship, a 120-gun battleship, was part of the Anglo-French fleet which entered the Baltic in the summer of 1854 and conducted a series of limited actions against Russian shipping and shore installations. By this time H.M.S. *St George* was obsolete; the Royal Navy was already commissioning and using battleships of similar outward appearance but with steam engines, funnels and screw propellers.

80. H.M.S. Duke of Wellington c. 1890 *(Anonymous)*

H.M.S. *Duke of Wellington* was the flagship for Admiral Sir Charles Napier during the first Baltic expedition of 1854 and for his successor, Admiral Dundas, for the second in 1855. Launched in 1852, the *Duke of Wellington* was a wooden, steam- and sail-powered battleship with a weight of 3,700 tons and a maximum speed of just over 10 knots. She carried 131 guns in three decks, of which 16 were 8-inch muzzle-loaders, one a 68-pound carronade and the rest 32-pounders. Her crew numbered 1100 officers and men.

In external appearances, the *Duke of Wellington* resembles the *St George* (**79**) save for her thin funnel (just behind the first mast). Within five years she would be rendered obsolete with the commissioning of H.M.S. *Warrior*, the first ironclad battleship.

81. Officers and crew of H.M.S. James Watt *(Anonymous)*

Launched in 1853, the *James Watt* was a steam- and sail-driven battleship with a speed of 11 knots and an armament of 91 guns. Like the *Duke of Wellington*, she served in both the Baltic expeditions.

Seated, cross-legged are a number of mid-shipmen, some probably boys of twelve or thirteen years who had just joined the navy. The presence of bearded officers suggests that the picture was taken after 1854 before which facial hair was frowned upon by the Admiralty (see **85**).

82. Warship deck c. 1850 *(Anonymous)*

To judge by this officer's uniform, if not his beard, this photograph shows the deck of a British Warship of the early 1850s. The guns are 32-pounders, smooth-bore cannon firing either solid shot or shell, which were the standard armament of British battleships during the Crimea (see **79** and **80**). Guns like this were used during the bombardment of Sebastopol by the navy in 1854 when British fire was seen to have a disappointing effect on the Russian defences. Within a few years of the Crimea, there would be a revolution in gunnery which led to the adoption of breech-loading, rifled cannon. The cannon in this picture together with the rigging suggest a scene which could easily have been taken in Nelson's time.

83. Admiral Sir Robert Lambert Baynes (1796–1869) *(Anonymous)*

Admiral Baynes, who had been promoted Lieutenant in 1818 and had seen action at the battle of Navarino in 1827, flew his flag in the paddle-steamer *Retribution* during the 1855 Baltic expedition. He also commanded a small squadron which cut out and destroyed Russian shipping in the Gulf of Bothnia in August 1855. Like many of the senior admirals, Baynes was an elderly man during the Crimean campaign. The long years of peace had created a naval gerontocracy which resembled its army counterpart and was reflected in the timidity of command during both Baltic expeditions.

84. Admiral Sir John Commerell V.C. (1829–1901) *(Anonymous)*

As a mid-shipman of 13, Commerell saw action during the China War of 1842. He was a Lieutenant on H.M.S. *Vulture* during Baltic operations in 1854 and in 1855 commanded H.M.S. *Weser* during the campaign in the Sea of Azov. Here, he commanded a landing party which made a dangerous march across country and burnt stocks of corn and forage. For this daring raid, he and two seamen were awarded the Victoria Cross. On a larger scale the successful naval and land operations on the Sea of Azov and its adjacent coastline were a demonstration of Allied sea power and a means of depriving the Russian field army in the Crimea of its supplies.

85. Lieutenant Montagu Reilly, R.N. *(Fenton)*

Lieutenant Reilly's ship, H.M.S. *Retribution*, had been part of the Allied fleet which entered the Black Sea in January 1854 and was entrusted with the message to the Russians at Sebastopol which warned them of the danger of interference with Allied and Turkish vessels. Whilst there, Lieutenant Reilly produced sketches and plans of the Russian fortifications – the rolled paper on the table beside him. Lieutenant Reilly sports a fine set of 'heavy swell' side-whiskers, something of a novelty for naval officers and one which provoked official wrath. When a whiskered officer boldly entered the Admiralty with despatches from the Baltic expedition, the First Sea Lord, white with anger and amazement, ordered him out with a wave of the hand and the tart comment 'Horseguards next door!' Yet just as the Horse Guards had reluctantly yielded on the beard and moustache issue, so did the navy, as Lieutenant Reilly's photograph suggests.

Notes to the Introduction

1. Quoted in H. and A. Gernsheim, *Roger Fenton, Photographer of the Crimean War* (London, 1954) p. 52.
2. Ed. P. Warner, *The Fields of War* (London, 1977) p. 148.
3. Quoted in J. Maas, *Victorian Painters* (London, 1969) p. 190.
4. H. and A. Gernsheim, *op. cit.*, p. 11.
5. For this and what follows, Constantin Savulĕscu, 'The First War Photographic Reportage', *Image*, 16 (1973) 13–16, and Constantin Savulĕscu, 'Early Photography in Eastern Europe: Romania', *History of Photography*, I (1977) 63–77.
6. For this and what follows, B. A. and H. K. Henisch, 'Robertson of Constantinople', *Image*, 17 (1974) 1–11.
7. H. and A. Gernsheim, *op. cit.*, p. 87
8. T. Gowing, *A Soldier's Experience or a Voice from the Ranks* (Nottingham, 1895) p. 11.
9. G. Lawson, *Surgeon in the Crimea* ed. V. Bonham-Carter (London, 1968) pp. 160–1.
10. J. A. Ewart, *The Story of a Soldier's Life* (London, 1881) I, 409–10.
11. Quoted in L. M. Case, *French Opinion on War and Diplomacy during the Second Empire* (New York, 1972) p. 28.
12. Quoted in H. Strachan, 'Soldiers, Strategy and Sebastopol', *The Historical Journal* 21, 1 (1978) 303–25.
13. E.g. in C. Hibbert, *The Destruction of Lord Raglan* (London, 1961) and W. Baring Pemberton, *Battles of the Crimean War* (London, 1962).
14. Quoted in A. Seaton, *The Crimean War; a Russian Chronicle* (London, 1976) pp. 176–7.
15. Ed. Marquess of Anglesey, *Little Hodge* (London, 1971) p. 71.
16. Diary entry for 23 November 1854 quoted in H. Troyat, *Tolstoy* (Penguin, 1970) p. 165.
17. Marquess of Anglesey, *A History of the British Cavalry (1851–1870)* (London, 1975) p. 103.
18. F. Stephenson, *At Home and on the Battlefield* (London, 1915) p. 146.
19. R. Portal, *Letters from the Crimea, 1854–56* (Winchester, 1900) p. 138.
20. Quoted in V. Bonham-Carter, *Soldier True* (London, 1963) p. 30.
21. W. M. Thackeray, *The Book of Snobs*, in *Collected Works* (London 1899) IX, 36.
22. *The Fields of War*, pp. 161–2.
23. W. M. Thackeray, *op. cit.*, pp. 33–4.
24. T. Gowing, *op. cit.*, p. 103 where he claimed that 'excessive drinking' caused much of the sickness during the winter of 1854–5.
25. National Army Museum 7606 (Scraps from a Corporal's Note Book Rough and Unvarnished) fo. 45.

Sources of Quotations

UNPRINTED

Daniel Bourke, Memoires (National Army Museum 6807–152).
Captain Cuninghame, Letters 1854–56.
John Fisher, Scraps from a Corporal's Note Book Rough and Unvarnished (National Army Museum 7606–38 and 39).
Charles Milligan, Letters (National Army Museum 6807–4)

PRINTED

J. Adye, *A Review of the Crimean War* (London, 1860)

R. Biddulph, The Fall of Sebastopol: a contemporary account, ed. H. Biddulph, *Journal of the Society for Army Historical Research* 19 (1940) 197–9.

Lady Alicia Blackwood, *A Narrative of a Residence on the Bosphorous Throughout the Crimean War* (London, 1881).

General Cathcart on beards, *Journal of the Society for Army Historical Research* 18 (1939) p. 132.

S. Calthorpe, *Cadogan's Crimea* (London, 1979).

John and Robert Campbell, *Letters from the Crimea* (Camberwell, 1979).

H. Clifford, *Henry Clifford V.C., his letters and sketches from the Crimea* (London, 1956).

G. Evelyn, *A Diary of the Crimea*, ed. C. Falls (London, 1954).

J. A. Ewart, *The Story of a Soldier's Life*, (2 volumes, London, 1881).

R. Fenton, Letters quoted in H. and A. Gernsheim, Roger Fenton, *Photographer of the Crimean War* (London, 1954).

Temple Godman, *The Fields of War*, ed. P. Warner (London, 1977).

T. Gowing, *A Soldier's Experience or a Voice from the Ranks* (Nottingham, 1895).

N. Kingscote, quoted in C. Hibbert, *The Destruction of Lord Raglan* (London, 1961) p. 28 n.

E. Hodge, *Little Hodge*, ed. Marquess of Anglesey (London, 1971).

G. Lawson, *Surgeon in the Crimea*, ed. V. Bonham-Carter (London, 1968).

G. Paget, *The Light Brigade in the Crimea* (London, 1881).

R. Portal, *Letters from the Crimea, 1854–56* (Winchester, 1900).

J. Robertson, *Personal Adventures and Anecdotes of an Old Officer* (London, 1906).

F. Stephenson, *At Home and on the Battlefield* (London, 1915).

R. Tylden, ed. G. Tylden, 'A Royal Engineer in the Crimea', *Journal of the Society for Army Historical Research*, 18 (1939) 23–6.

C. E. Trevelyan, *Civil Administration of the Army*, 1 May 1855 (Confidential Memorandum) where H. W. Gordon's letter is printed.

E. Wood, *From Midshipman to Field Marshall* (London, 1907).

ADDITIONAL BIBLIOGRAPHY

K. Chesney, *A Crimean War Reader* (London, 1960).

W. L. Clowes, *The Royal Navy* (7 volumes, London, 1897–1903).

N. Gash, *Aristocracy and People, Britain 1815–65* (London, 1979).

A. W. Kinglake, *The Invasion of the Crimea* (8 volumes, London 1863–87).

H. Oake-Jones, 'Photography in the Crimea', *Journal of the Society for Army Historical Research*, 18 and 19 (1939 and 1940).

E. M. Speirs, *The Army and Society, 1815–1914* (London, 1980).

The author and publishers would like to thank the following for permission to quote from their works:

A. Seaton: *The Crimean War: a Russian Chronicle*, B. T. Batsford Ltd

P. Warner (ed): *The Fields of War*, John Murray (Publishers) Ltd

C. Fales (ed): *A Diary of the Crimea*, Gerald Duckworth & Co Ltd

V. Bonham-Carter (ed): *Surgeon in the Crimea*, Constable & Co Ltd

H. Troyat: *Tolstoy*, Doubleday & Co, Inc.

The Marquess of Anglesey (ed): *Little Hodge*, Leo Cooper Ltd

Index

RUSSIA

AUSTRIAN
EMPIRE

Moldavia

Odessa

Caspian Sea

Wallachia

Crimea

Bucharest

Sebastopol

Sea of Azov

River
Danube

Silistria

Varna

Black Sea

TURKISH

Constantinople

The Straits

Scutari

Sinope

EMPIRE

Aegean Sea

0   200

GREECE

miles

Katcha B.

Black Sea

Environs of
SEBASTOPOL
Circa 1854

0   1   2   3   4   5

Miles